Russia: *The* Challenge *of* Change
Russie : *le* défi *d'une* métamorphose

Russia: *The* Challenge *of* Change
Russie : *le* défi *d'une* métamorphose

**Proceedings from the International Symposium
held at Glendon College, York University, March 1 2003,
including
essays written by members of the
Russia Independent Study Committee**

**Papers assembled and edited by Carlos Canales,
Lilly A. Lo Manto, and Sergei Plekhanov**

**Glendon College, York University
Toronto, Ontario, Canada
January 2004**

Glendon College, York University
2275 Bayview Avenue, Toronto, ON M4N 3M6

Published in Toronto in 2004
Copyright 2004 The authors and editors

The Russia Independent Study Committee:
Christopher Baker
Carlos Canales
Edith da Costa
Kristell Dortel
Eugene Galaev
Eugene Kvache
Lilly A. Lo Manto

Editing: Carlos Canales, Lilly A. Lo Manto, and Sergei Plekhanov
Editorial assistance: Christopher Baker and Eugene Kvache
Layout: Christopher Baker, Carlos Canales, and Edith da Costa
Cover: Kristell Dortel

For orders, please contact: conference_publication@gl.yorku.ca

ISBN: 1-55014-435-9

Printed and bound in Canada by
The University of Toronto Press

Preface

For the past eight years, senior students from Glendon College, York University have been committed to a very unique and innovative annual conference project. This student-led initiative has become a well-respected tradition at Glendon College, entailing, each year, the study of a particular country or region of the world chosen by the students. For the academic year 2002-2003, our Student Committee chose Russia as the theme for this project.

Indisputably, Russia has baffled its citizens and foreigners alike throughout the twists and turns of its tumultuous history. In the past one hundred years, the Russian people have experienced a revolution, two world wars, seven decades of communist rule, and an ideological confrontation with the West. In 1991, the Russian Federation emerged as one of the fifteen 'new' nations, after the collapse of the Soviet Union. During the past twelve years, this country has faced immense challenges in transforming itself from an 'authoritarian' regime, with a centrally planned economy, into a 'free-market' democracy. Today, Russia is the largest country in the world, a major political player in the global arena, and a state with immense economic potential. Russia possesses prodigious natural resources, a key geopolitical position as a bridge between Europe and Asia, and international influence as one of the major powers. Given Russia's importance on the world stage, it is critical to understand where Russia stands today and where it is headed in the future.

Having this in mind, we decided to commemorate Russia by hosting an International Symposium entitled "Russia: The Challenge of Change", which took place on March 1, 2003 at Glendon College. Our Committee now proudly presents in this work the proceedings of this conference along with some of our essays.

In this text, a number of challenges that Russia is subject to are examined. Contributors to the first section examine the interactions between tradition and reform in the Russian historical experience. In the second section, political and economic issues are examined, specifically problems associated with building a democratic state and a market economy. Contributors to the third section comment on Russia's external affairs, namely Russia-Canada relations, her role on the international scene, and current trends in her foreign policy.

We hope this will contribute to a better understanding of Russia's internal and foreign affairs, while stimulating further discussion on the possible directions Russia may take in the future. Moreover, we would like this discussion to contribute to the strengthening of Canada-Russia relations. But most importantly, we would like Russia to take the path that best provides peace, stability, and prosperity for the future of her people.

Carlos Canales and Lilly A. Lo Manto

Acknowledgements

We greatly appreciate the help of the following individuals, without whose guidance and support this project would have not been possible:

Professor Sergei Plekhanov who taught us a seminar course on Russia and worked as faculty advisor to the Conference project and as Co-Editor of this book; Professor Domenico Mazzeo, who graciously contributed his time to ensuring the overall success of the project; Professor Kenneth McRoberts, who provided tremendous assistance in securing the participation of notable speakers, while ensuring logistical support for the Conference; and all of the panellists, whose participation ensured an event filled with lively discussion and debate, as well as to those who graciously provided us with their written works.

Moreover, we are grateful for the generous financial contributions without which the symposium and this publication would have never been realized. Lastly, we wish to acknowledge all those who supported us throughout the yearlong preparations and helped us to complete this project.

Sponsors

The Russia Independent Study Committee would like to thank the following organizations for their financial assistance:

Canadian Defence and Foreign Affairs Institute
http://www.cdfai.org/

Canadian Institute of International Affairs
http://www.ciia.org/

Canada Russia Business Forum
http://www.canada-russia.com/

Department of Foreign Affairs and International Trade
http://www.dfait-maeci.gc.ca/

Office of the Principal, Glendon College
http://www.glendon.yorku.ca

Office of Student Affairs, Glendon College
http://www.glendon.yorku.ca

YCISS Post Communist Studies Programme
http://www.yorku.ca/yciss/

Office of the Vice-President of International Affairs, York University
http://international.yorku.ca

Table of Contents

Contributors

Carlos Canales
The Russian Presidency and the Process of Democratization

Carlos Canales completed an Honours B.A. in International Studies and a consecutive Degree in Political Science at Glendon College, York University. He is currently pursuing a M.A. in International Politics and International Law at l'Université du Québec à Montréal. His academic interests include Comparative Politics, Regional Integration, Public International Law, and International Development/Human Rights.

His Excellency Vitaly Churkin
Canada-Russia Relations: A Russian View

Vitaly Churkin holds a Ph.D. in International Relations. As a career diplomat since 1974, he has served in the Soviet and Russian Ministries of Foreign Affairs in a number of ranking posts, including those of Director of the Information Department, Deputy Minister, and Russian President's Special Envoy to Yugoslavia. His foreign postings have included the USSR Embassy in Washington, and the Russian Embassy in Brussels, where he served as Russian Ambassador to Belgium as well as Liaison Ambassador to NATO and WEU. Dr. Churkin has served as Russia's Ambassador to Canada from 1998 to 2003.

Joan DeBardeleben
Public Attitudes, Democracy, and Elections in Russia

Joan DeBardeleben is a Professor of Political Science at Carleton University. She holds a Ph.D. from the University of Wisconsin-Madison. Recently, she has become engaged in survey research in Russia. From 1993 to 1997, she organized a training course for Russian sociologists in the conduct of survey research (funded by CIDA). Most recently, Professor DeBardeleben has undertaken research on Russian attitudes toward privatization and towards federalism. She is also the

Russia project director for a study of labour-management relations and
Russian work attitudes in Russian enterprises, carried out in conjunction
with the Institute of Sociology of the Russian Academy of Sciences.
Until 2003, Professor DeBardeleben served as Director of the Centre for
European and Russian Studies at Carleton University.

Georgi Derluguian
A Cyclical Theory of Russia's Historical Change

Georgi Derluguian holds a MA and Ph.D. in Sociology from Moscow
State University. He has authored a micro-sociological study of
Mozambique's guerrilla wars as well as studies of insurgencies and
ethnic conflicts in Post-Soviet Caucasus. Since 1990, he has worked with
Immanuel Wallerstein at the Fernand Braudel Center of Binghamton
University. He is currently an assistant professor of sociology at
Northwestern University. In November 2003, Verso (London) published
his book *Bourdieu's Secret Admirer in the Caucasus: A World-Systemic
Ethnography of Post-Communism*.

Honorable Bill Graham
Canada-Russia Relations: A Canadian View

First elected as Member of Parliament for Toronto Centre-Rosedale in
1993, Bill Graham was appointed Minister of Foreign Affairs in January
2002. From 1995 to 2002, Mr. Graham served as Chairman of the House
of Commons Standing Committee on Foreign Affairs and International
Trade. Under his Chairmanship, the Committee produced important
reports on issues including Canada's interests in the World Trade
Organization, Canada's role in Kosovo, the implementation of legislation
for the International Criminal Court, and the Summit of the Americas in
Quebec City. Active in international parliamentary associations, Mr.
Graham was elected founding President of the Inter-Parliamentary
Forum of the Americas. He has served as Vice-President and Treasurer
of the Parliamentary Association of the Organization for Security and
Cooperation in Europe, and as Treasurer of Liberal International. Mr.
Graham obtained a doctorate in law from the University of Paris.

Robert Johnson
Can Russia Be Reformed?

Robert Johnson's research concentrates on social and economic questions. He is the author of *Peasant and Proletarian: Moscow's Working Class at the End of the Nineteenth Century* (1979), and co-author of *The Seam Allowance: Industrial Homework in Canada's Garment Industry* (1982). He also edited *A Half-Century of Silence: The 1937 Census of USSR* (Russian Studies in History, Summer 1992). From 1993 through to 2001, he served as Principal Investigator of the Stalin Era Research and Archives Project. His own focus within that collaborative project was on the population of the USSR in the 1920s and 1930s. He has written on labour and labour unrest, peasant family life, and other social and economic issues. He is a frequent commentator for Canadian news media on current events in Russia and the former Soviet Union. From 1989 to 2001 he served as Director of the Centre for Russian and East European Studies (University of Toronto).

Eugene Kvache
Eurasianism in Russian Foreign Policy

Eugene Kvache is working towards an Honours Degree in International Studies and Political Science. His academic interests are centered on security and defence aspects of Canadian foreign policy. His research focuses on the nature of Russia-Canada relations and the implications of changes in Russia, for Canadian national security.

Anne Leahy
"Oumom Rossiyou Nie Poniat…"

Anne Leahy is a Canadian diplomat who has spent several years in Eastern Europe. Her first assignment in Moscow was First Secretary (internal affairs), in the Canadian Embassy to the USSR, in the early eighties. She returned to Eastern Europe as Ambassador to Poland, from 1993 to 1996, and to Russia (concurrently to Armenia, Belarus and Uzbekistan), from 1996 to 1999. In the Department of Foreign Affairs and International Trade, she headed the Policy Planning Bureau from 1992 to 1993. Ms. Leahy became the first Director of the Institute d'Études internationales de Montréal, created in October 2002, at l'Université de Québec à Montréal.

Lilly A. Lo Manto
Causes of Failure: Why Russia's Oil Industry Did Not Attract Large Scale Foreign Investment?

Lilly A. Lo Manto is a fourth year Honours International Studies Major. Lilly's academic interests include Public International Law, Political Economy, and Canadian Foreign Investment in Europe and the former Soviet Union. Upon graduation, she wishes to pursue joint legal and graduate studies.

Sergei Plekhanov
Who Drives the Troika?
Continuity and Change in Russian Foreign Policy

Sergei M. Plekhanov holds a B.A. and a M.A. in International Relations from Moscow State Institute of International Relations (1968) and a Ph.D. in History from the Institute for the Study of the USA and Canada, Academy of Sciences of the USSR. From 1988 to 1993, he served as a Deputy Director of the Institute. Dr. Plekhanov has taught as Visiting Professor at the University of California, Irvine, and Occidental College (Los Angeles), and worked as Soviet Affairs Consultant with CBS News (1989-1991). Since his arrival in Canada, in 1993, he has been a frequent commentator on Russian and East European affairs for Canadian Television, radio networks and print media. Currently Sergei Plekhanov is an Associate Professor at the Department of Political Science, York University, a Coordinator of the Post-Communist Studies Program at York Centre for International and Security Studies, and a Senior Associate of the Centre for Russian and East European Studies, University of Toronto.

Richard Pope
Cracking the Enigma Code: Russia's Usable Past

Richard Pope is a professor of Russian Literature and culture at York University. He pursued M.A., Certificate, and Ph.D studies at Columbia University. Pope taught at Indiana University and University of Virginia before coming to York in 1973. His publications are mainly about Russian mediaeval literature and Russian literature of the nineteenth and twentieth century. His most recent work is on the cultural history of St Petersburg paper at Tampere and publication in the proceedings of the conference: *Petersburg Apocalyptic: Beauty and the Beast.*

Vladimir Popov
Circumstances Versus Policy Choices: Why Has Economic Performance of FSU States Been so Poor?

Vladimir Popov holds Ph.D.s (Candidate of Science, 1980; and Doctor of Science, 1990) from the Institute of the US and Canada of the Academy of Sciences of the USSR. He is currently the Sector Head at the Academy of the National Economy in Moscow, professor at the New Economic School in Moscow, and visiting professor at Carleton University in Ottawa. From 1996 to 1998, Vlademir Popov was a Senior Research Fellow in the World Institute for Development Economics Research of the United Nations University (WIDER/UNU) in Helsinki, Finland, co-directing a project entitled "Transition Strategies, Alternatives and Outcomes". He has taught in Finland, Germany, Italy, Russia, Sweden and the United States.

Peter H. Solomon, Jr.
Reforming Russia's Judiciary

Peter H. Solomon, Jr., is Professor of Political Science, Law and Criminology as well as Director of the Centre for Russian and East European Studies at the University of Toronto. His recent publications include: *Soviet Criminal Justice under Stalin* (Cambridge U. Press, 1996); *Reforming Justice in Russia, 1864-1996* (edited; M.E. Sharpe, 1997); *Courts and_Transition in Russia: The Challenge of Judicial Reform* (with Todd Foglesong; Westview, 2000); and "Putin's Judicial

Reform: Making Judges Accountable as well as Independent," *East European Constitutional Review* (Winter/Spring, 2002). He is an active participant in judicial reform programs in the Russian Federation and other post-Soviet states.

Valerie Sperling
Engendering Democracy in Russia

Valerie Sperling is Assistant Professor in the Department of Government and International Relations at Clark University (Worcester, MA). She received her Ph.D. from the University of California, Berkeley. Valerie Sperling's publications include *Organizing Women in Contemporary Russia* (Cambridge University Press, 1999) and several articles on gender politics in Russia. Her edited volume, *Building the Russian State: Institutional Crisis and the Quest for Democratic Governance*, was published by Westview Press in 2000. Sperling is currently working on a new book on the effects of globalization on liberal democratic state-building.

Nikolai V. Zlobin
Russia's Place in the Emerging World Order

Dr. Zlobin is at the Centre for Defense Information in Washington DC, as a Senior Fellow and Director of Russian and Asian Programs. He is a leading scholar of U.S.-Russian relations as well as Russian, Eurasian and regional politics, history and international security. Dr. Zlobin also edits and directs the CDI Project Washington Profile, a Russian language international news and analysis agency. The online service is designed to support freedom of information in Russia and other former Soviet Union countries, Dr. Zlobin writes a regular column for the Russian daily *Izvestia* and has been a special correspondent to *Literaturnaya Gazeta*, *Obshchaya Gazeta*, and *Nezavisimaya Gazeta*. He is the executive editor of *Demokratizatsiya*, an academic journal devoted to study of problems of post-communist change. He received his Ph.D. in History from Moscow State University.

Foreword

Glendon College's founding Principal was Escott Reid. Rhodes Scholar, former high commissioner to India and ambassador to Western Germany, Reid was one of the artisans of Canada's post World War II foreign policy. Within his vision, Glendon College was to be devoted to preparing Canadians for public service. It was for this reason that the college was made a fully bilingual campus: all graduates were to be competent in Canada's second official language. For, reflecting Reid's own experience and preoccupations, the notion of public affairs involved international as well as domestic matters.

Au fil des ans, l'enseignement bilingue en sciences sociales et lettres de Glendon a mené bon nombre d'étudiants à jouer un rôle de premier plan au niveau des relations internationales. On compte parmi nos anciens et anciennes trois ambassadeurs du Canada, un Secrétaire-Général-adjoint (Amnistie internationale), des économistes de réputation internationale, ainsi que beaucoup d'autres personnes de haut calibre occupant ou ayant occupé des postes d'importance à l'échelle mondiale.

Notre programme d'études internationales exerce une influence prépondérante dans la préparation des étudiants de Glendon à la vie publique internationale. Pluridisciplinaire, ce programme s'appui sur l'ensemble des ressources du Collège pour offrir une formation unique dans les deux langues officielles du Canada et ce, dans le domaine des études internationales.

One of the programs most remarkable achievements is the organization by its students of annual conferences. This is the eighth such conference. The topics of previous conferences were, in chronological order: Cuba, China, South Africa, the European Union, the Middle East, South East Asia, Brazil, and Russia. In most instances, the conferences have been followed by visits to the region in question. The students have already chosen the theme for next year's conference: India.

So, as Principal of Glendon, I am delighted to declare open the conference on "Russia: The Challenge of Change – Russie: Le défi d'une métamorphose"

Professor Kenneth McRoberts
Principal of Glendon College, York University

Section 1

Can Russia Change?

Can Russia Be Reformed?

Professor Robert Johnson, University of Toronto

I've entitled my remarks today "Can Russia Be Reformed?" The fast and dirty answer to this question – what might be called the Bill Clinton answer – is: 'Define reform'. I'm going to argue that the entire history of Russia from the earliest times can be viewed as the history of reform – of almost incessant, deliberate efforts to alter institutions, habits, cultures, modes of governance. Indisputably, Ivan IV's Oprichnina was a reform, as were the Westernization program of Peter I, the agricultural collectivization and industrialization drive of the 1930s, the Khrushchev post-Stalin 'Thaw', the Brezhnev counter-Thaw, and the Yeltsin constitution of 1993.

This doesn't mean, however, that all those efforts were successful or instrumental or that they achieved the results for which they were designed. A quick overview of some of the more spectacular reform efforts of past ages will, I think, suggest some lessons or cautions for present and future reformers.

The Westernization of Peter I is a good place to begin, not least because its most tangible manifestation, the city that bears Peter's name, is celebrating its three hundredth anniversary, this year. Peter's accomplishments are reflected today in the canals of St. Petersburg, the Italianate palaces, the broad boulevards, the manufacturing and commerce of one of the world's great cities. Foreigners make a beeline for the Hermitage, with its spectacular collection of mostly western European art. Most westerners have heard the legends of how Peter shaved off the beards of traditionalists, how he travelled to Amsterdam to learn carpentry and navigation, how he introduced Western modes of dress and behaviour to his country. And, of course, how he defeated most of his enemies and enlarged his country's borders.

What we hear less about is how these results were achieved, at what price. If we look for Peter's legacy in the mines of the Ural mountains or in the serf-powered agricultural estates of central Russia, if we could excavate beneath the palaces to find the skeletons of all the involuntary laborers who died while building Peter's city in the muddy swamp of the Neva's estuary, we get a different picture. Peter reformed Russia by using the tools and materials that were closest at hand, and these were mainly tools of coercion. I don't mean to suggest that Russia was unique in taxing and coercing its subjects, or that there are no skeletons beneath Paris or London. But it seems to me that there is a paradox to Peter's reforms that often goes unnoticed: In making Russia more 'modern' and western, Peter also reinforced its most traditional and, if you will, backward features. The serfs who made up the vast majority of his country's population ended up more exploited, more tightly bound to their masters and their duties and their social station, than they had been before Peter's reign. In an age when serfdom was fading away in much of western Europe, Peter consolidated and solidified it, and it endured for almost 150 years after his death.

Can we draw a conclusion? A Reform, it seems, comes at a price that isn't always recognized or remembered. In Peter's case, it left a legacy of problems (of serfdom and related oppression) that in the long run held Russia back, and ultimately worked against the very westernization that Peter was trying to implement.

The next reform, I would like to address is the one Russians traditionally referred to as the 'Great Reform' – the package of changes introduced early in the reign of Alexander II (1855-1881), foremost among them the emancipation of the serfs. This is another story that will be familiar to most readers, and in some ways it is a story of success. More than one writer has noted the contrast between Russia, where emancipation was achieved with a minimum of social disruption and bloodshed, and the United States, where slavery was ended only after a fratricidal Civil War that cost hundreds of thousands of lives. Russia's emancipation, moreover, was part of a package of reforms that also created new, representative institutions of local government (the 'zemstvo') and liberalized the judiciary, military service, censorship, urban administration, higher education, and many other areas of political and economic life.

What isn't always appreciated, however, is that virtually all of these reforms produced results that the tsar and his ministers had not anticipated. Perhaps, the most dramatic example came at the trial of the radical populist Vera Zasulich for attempting to assassinate a prominent police official in 1878. Under the newly-reformed court procedures, her lawyers used the public trial as a forum for denouncing repressive police practices, and the jury – another innovation – acquitted Zasulich. From that point onward, Russian police agencies tried to bypass the courts and rely more upon extra-judicial methods of investigation and punishment. If they couldn't undo the reform, they did their best to circumvent it.

In later years other reforms of the early 1860s, such as the 'zemstvo' and university statutes, were formally reversed by counter-reforms. Peasant emancipation was fully implemented, but did not produce the economic or social stability that its architects had intended. Peasants resented the fact that they were obliged to repay the state, over a period of 49 years, for the land they received under emancipation. Another source of discontent was that their former lords retained control of large tracts of land. The peasant commune, which the reformers had considered a source of social stability, eventually became a nucleus for resistance and social unrest.

Does this mean that the 'Great Reform' was ill-conceived or unrealizable? I don't think so. What it does suggest, however, is that any reform is likely to take on a life of its own, producing unexpected results.

The object of reform is almost always a product of previous history, which will help to condition the reform's outcomes. Let me say this more concretely: The Russian countryside in 1861 was not a blank slate on which Alexander II and his ministers could write whatever they chose. Emancipation was an interactive process, in which the life that peasants had led under serfdom helped define the range of possible transformations.

The final decades of Romanov rule saw a still different array of reform initiatives, aimed at strengthening capitalist tendencies. These were associated with the names of two of the most prominent officials of the time, Sergius Witte and Petr Stolypin. Today, a hundred years later, both of these have become the object of much attention in Russia as representatives of 'alternatives' that could have taken Russia down a different path.

Witte served as Minister of Finance through most of the 1890s. He is credited with the construction of the Trans-Siberian railway and with a spurt of economic growth that had few equals anywhere in the world at that time. Because of time constraints, I can only mention a few key points in his career and reform strategy: 1) He recognized that Russia could not move forward by mechanically copying the policies of other industrial powers; instead he relied on a combination of high tariffs, active state intervention, and foreign investment; 2) the Trans-Siberian railroad was designed to enable Russia to expand its economic influence in China and the North Pacific region, where it could compete more effectively with the other European Great Powers of the day; 3) although he strongly opposed going to war against Japan, that disastrous war (1904-1905) was almost a direct outcome of his policies, in an indirect way, those same policies brought Russia into alliance with France and Britain, helping to pave the way to her disastrous involvement in the First World War; 4) his career was cut short when he lost the tsar's confidence – one feature of the Old Regime that was outside his power to change. Conclusions? Reforms are more likely to succeed when they are addressed to the specific circumstances and opportunities of a historical moment, without mechanically following a recipe from some other time and place. Reform is, however, a complex process whose outcomes cannot always be anticipated, or whose unwelcome outcomes cannot be prevented.

What about Stolypin? You may remember that he supported a program of land reform, based on the introduction of private ownership to the communally-organized peasantry. By the best estimates, roughly 25% of the peasants in the Empire underwent some kind of reorganization of their holdings, BUT 1) Stolypin lost the tsar's favor, and was assassinated by a terrorist before his program really took hold. 2) Historians today give the Stolypin program credit mainly for the ways in which it departed from its original agenda and adapted to peasant wishes and needs – an adaptation that was not Stolypin's work. 3) In 1917, as the Bolsheviks were coming to power, peasants throughout the empire strongly reasserted their communal instincts, and reversed the process of privatization. From then until 2002, full private ownership of land has not existed in Russia. The new Land Code passed last year is still being contested. In sum, the Stolypin experience suggests that reforms are more effective when they are flexible and responsive to circumstances. But unless an environment is favourable a program of reform can be reversed overnight.

Arguably the most ambitious and least successful reform of the Soviet era was agricultural collectivization. The campaign that Stalin inaugurated at the end of the 1920s shows a particular kind of hubris – of a set of leaders who thought that Marxism gave them a recipe for defeating class enemies and building a socialist future. The system that they built has been criticized not just for the enormous loss of life and resources that went into its construction, but also for the economic inefficiencies that plagued it from Day 1. Some of collectivization's proponents presented the reform as a means of introducing efficiency and economies of scale to peasant agriculture, but the inefficiencies of the kolkhoz system persisted to the very end of the Soviet Union. Others saw collectivization as a means of extracting an investable surplus from an unwilling countryside, but even in this regard it should probably be counted a failure: Faced with the disastrous harvests of the early years, the Soviet leadership had to divert resources into agriculture that they had hoped to use for industrial construction. In later years – the 1960s and beyond – agriculture remained a drain on the country's resources, and today the agricultural sector is still waiting for change. Collectivization illustrates what Anatolii Vishnevskii has called Aconservative modernization – perhaps a modern equivalent of what Peter I was seeking 300 years ago. This was an attempt to build a modern western and industrial society and economy without replicating the human and social infrastructure on which the Amodel societies rested. It didn't work.

The final reform on my list is the Yeltsin constitution of 1993. I can remember the debates that went on in that year, and the enthusiasm with which many western observers applauded President Yeltsin's attack on the Duma. What exactly was in the minds of the President's advisors I can not say, but I have a pretty clear recollection of the terms in which the discussion was framed in North America. Yeltsin, in the eyes of many westerners, was representing 'democracy' while the Duma members, although they had been popularly elected, were perceived as enemies of reform. In retrospect, the 1993 reform looks more like a response to the exigencies of one moment, based on little analysis of how that moment had come about. The result was not so much 'democracy' as an 'executive presidency' – a political system in which the President's powers are significantly greater than in most parliamentary regimes. Yeltsin himself was never wholly successful in using those powers, but his successor shows every sign of being able to put this machinery to more ambitious uses. Whether the ultimate result will be more democratic ones remains, I believe, an open question.

Are there overall lessons to this recital? It is tempting to say 'plus ça change', but I think we can do better than that. Certainly one moral is: 'Be careful what you wish for'. Most of the reforms on my list have produced at least some unexpected results, and most have carried price tags that were not clearly recognized at the time they were introduced.

Another moral, powerfully reinforced by the experiences of many other states and nations, is that bigger isn't usually better: the grander the scheme, the greater the potential for disaster. The reforms that have turned out to be most productive in the long run have usually begun with more modest goals and targets, and have been flexible enough to change course over time. The more rigidly a program was followed, the greater the chance of negative results and unexpected costs.

In this very brief and truncated presentation, I've been trying to toss out some ideas and problems that will help you to think about the topics that follow on today's agenda – reforms that have been attempted in the past few years, or are still being contemplated. I am tempted to conclude with a well-known quotation from Marx: "Men make their own history, but not in circumstances of their own choosing". I think, though, that Mick Jagger said it more succinctly: "You can't always get what you want, but if you *try try try*, you may sometimes get what you need".

Who Drives The Troika?
Professor Sergei Plekhanov, York University

As the conference brochure reminds us, Nikolai Gogol, writing a century and a half ago, compared Russia with a troika: a three-horse carriage rolling fast across the roadless, boundless, windswept Russian prairie – the steppe. "Oh, troika, birdlike troika, who has invented you? – he wrote. Only a very bold people could have created you in a land which does things in a big way and which has spread forth half around the world... The driver is not wearing some German boots – no, he's all beard and mittens, and he sits hell knows on what – but watch him get up, crack his whip, start his long song – and the horses shoot forward, the spokes in the wheels become smooth discs, and the pedestrian shrieks in fright – and there it flies!

Isn't it also you, Russia that is speeding forward like a boisterous, winning troika? Smoke clouds at your feet, bridges roll, and everything lags behind and stays in the past... What is the meaning of this horrifying movement? What mysterious force is hidden in these incredible horses? ...Where are you flying, Russia, answer me?.. No, she won't answer".[1]

This is an interesting comparison – especially if we recall that it described Russia in the middle of the 19th century, when the Europeans saw her, under the iron rule of Nicholas I, as a static, conservative, backward empire. Challenging this perception, and as if foreseeing the great upheavals ahead, Gogol pictured Russia as a country moving forward at great speed – but without a clear sense of where it is headed.

Sixteen years ago, when a young, confident, powerful General Secretary of the CPSU urged a stony-faced congress of his party to get Russia moving to catch up with the West, the main doubt was whether any serious, fundamental changes were at all possible in the enormous, inert bureaucratic empire built under the red flag. No one could imagine how much was to change. And the dominant discourse about Russia in these sixteen years has been dominated by the theme of incredible, earth-shaking, historic transformations – from communism to capitalism, from authoritarianism to democracy, from empire to nation-state, from atheism to revival of religion.

But after all these great transformations, one is left wondering whether Russia has become more like the West or more like its own traditional self. Look at the symbolic side. The Westernized Russia flies the tricolour flag of Peter the Great and wears the Byzantian state emblem with its double eagle, holy cross and scepter, 1,500 years old, with the superimposed old coat of arms of Muscovy, the Third Rome, 500 years old. While old churches are being restored and many new ones are being built, the Russian Army gets back its red flag and red star, and the new national anthem is the old Soviet one, with modified words, of course.

But is it a problem if Russia has revived its traditions while it was remaking itself in the Western image? Isn't it a measure of a country's inner strength and self-confidence if it adopts new and foreign ideas and practices creatively, grafting them on without damaging the native stem? Unfortunately, this is not exactly how we Russians do things – and the question is why.

Every country periodically has to deal with the challenge of change in one from or another. Some countries cope with the challenge by gradually modifying, reforming existing institutions in line with the changed circumstances. Others fail at reform and carry out the changes through the destruction of the existing order, chaos, and subsequent rebuilding. Looking back on the century which has seen more revolutions than any other, the story of Russian communism being at the center of it all – both in 1917 and in 1991 – a century which has celebrated revolution as the locomotive of history, it is easy to become a skeptic about revolutionary means. Indeed, evolution, carefully designed reform is obviously the preferred method, as human society is essentially organic, not mechanical. It is a persuasive argument that a revolution is a tragedy, a catastrophe, a form of cruel and unusual punishment – or an unaffordable luxury, if you will. As the ancient Chinese curse put it, 'May you live in interesting times'.

As a Russian, I have lived through incredibly interesting times, taking part in the Soviet reform process, and then in the revolutionary events which culminated in the collapse of the Soviet system. I've experienced an intoxicating sense of liberation after the defeat of the hardline coup in August of 1991 – but that sense was mixed with deep anxiety about the consequences of 'destroying a state': we can not live without a state, how can we rebuild it? Looking back at what happened next, I conclude that by failing at gradual, evolutionary transformation of the old order, and by opting to go through the agony of destruction followed by chaos, followed by the beginning of a very difficult recovery, Russia has remained true to its old self.

Among the 27 countries of Eastern Europe and the former Soviet Union, those that have been transformed along Western lines with relatively more success and at relatively less cost, are those where elements of the Western model were already in place – market economy, civil society, political pluralism. For the Czechs or the Hungarians, the logic of the market economy and the language of civil society are familiar, traditional things. What it means is that large numbers of people in such a society have at their disposal the mechanisms, the knowledge, and the habits to participate in the process of change. And the wider the active community, the more circumspect the rulers, the more consensual the decision-making, the more concern about the costs of change.

The Russian traditions are different, of course. The main agency of change in Russia has always been the state, not the people. If the people do become politically active, it is usually to protest against the actions of the state, or to overthrow the state altogether. The people do have strong democratic values – but they don't have much chance to practice them in day-to-day political life. Contemporary Russia is marked by a sense of remarkable disappointment with politics as a meaningful, effective citizen action. This leaves the government quite free to govern as it sees fit – but at the same time quite limited in its ability to affect what goes on in society. Russia demonstrates, albeit in new forms, traditional alienation between the rulers and the ruled. The rulers, instinctively preferring command to consultation, issue orders, which regularly fail to be implemented. The people feign obedience, a time-tested survival technique, while doing everything possible to do things their own way. In the past, this mutual alienation has not prevented the people and the rulers from coming together strongly in cases of war – but it has arguably been a major cause of the chronic inefficiency of the institutions of civilian life.

The way Russia was transformed in the 1990s was deeply traditional: a top-down, elite-driven overhaul of social relations with society's role being that of a mostly passive object, raw material for the new system – and the bearer of the huge costs of change. The reformers had a program, and the personality of Boris Yeltsin symbolized a determination to implement it quickly, at all costs, overcoming resistance by all means available. It has been aptly termed 'Market Bolshevism'.[2] In the early nineties, Russian debates on the speed of change were conducted in the form of discussing the question: "Which is the more humane way of chopping off a cat's tail – bit by bit, or in one chop?" In late 1990s, cruelty to animals was criminalized in Russia, but the poor cat had already suffered. In China, reformers also used the cat's image to make their point, but in a markedly different way: "It doesn't matter what colour is the cat, so long as it catches the mice".

Russian Westernizers, as well as many Western champions of Russia's recent reforms, have bemoaned Russia's resistance to the reform project. But actually, the reforms of the past decade have revealed a strong convergence between the neoliberal orthodoxy, with its insistence on the liberation of market forces, and the authoritarian traditions of the Russian state. The orthodoxy could only be enforced in Russia by authoritarian means. And the Russian elites have benefited from the process so massively – at the expense of the masses of citizens – that one almost begins to suspect that the so-called 'Washington consensus' was drafted in the Kremlin, not in Washington.

These days, Russia finds itself in a conservative pause after a decade and a half of exhausting changes. The troika is tired. The country looks more stable and less disorderly. But few would venture to say that a sustainable new political-economic system is already in place in Russia. The new system is still an unfinished product, a mix of old and new elements that works in some areas and is deeply dysfunctional in others. More changes are inevitable. And the crucial question is what role Russian citizens will play in the changes, which are bound to come.

It is hard to imagine them remaining in the role of passive onlookers and patient followers of the elites. Russian society is only beginning to adapt to the new conditions in which it finds itself. The Russians have political and civic freedoms on a scale historically unprecedented for Russia – and the harsh challenges of the market economy force them to defend their interests as best they can.

In Gogol's troika, the people are obviously in the role of the horses. Perhaps, Russia will have a better sense of where it is going – and become more predictable, – when its people, at long last, assume the role of the driver.

I would like to conclude with a few quotes from the politicians of the new Russia. They evoke the memory of the great Russian satirist, Saltykov- Shchedrin, whose portraits of Russian officialdom, drawn in the middle of the 19th century, look as if they had been painted today. Here is a sampling of Russian politicians' tribute to the great satirist:[3]

Alexander Zaveryukha, Minister of Agriculture, Feb. 1994:
"Russia must feed its farmers".

Sergei Kalashnikov, Minister of Labour, July 2000:
"In 1999, we have managed to reduce the numbers of pensioners by nearly 700,000 people".

Ilya Klebanov, Minister of Defence Industry, Oct. 1999:

"The defence industry is not any different from the bicycle industry, because bicycles have always been produced by the defence industry".

Yuri Maslyukov, Vice Prime Minister, Mar. 1999, in response to the question about the amount of money Russia received from the IMF:

"This is a great secret, because even I don't know exactly how much".

Prime Minister Sergei Stepashin, May 1999:

"The improvement of the people's life, which has been achieved at the expense of the sharp fall of their living standards, will continue to advance".

Alexander Shokhin, MP, April 2000

"We must move back from the brink of the abyss at the bottom of which we find ourselves".

Yegor Stroev, Speaker of the Russian Federation Council, Jan. 1999:

"Who is saying this? Today, people talk too much. Me, I prefer to listen to those who don't say anything".

Vladimir Ustinov, Prosecutor General, Nov. 2001:

"Every lawbreaker works in a specific government ministry".

Yegor Stroev, Speaker of the Russian Federation Council, Sept. 2000:
"There are many intelligent people in the Federation Council today, but the public has many doubts as to how they got there".

Vladimir Potanin, banker, April 1999:
"A businessman doesn't know himself what is profitable for him. The government must give him some kind of guidance".

Ivan Anichkin, MP, Oct. 1999:
"Of two evils, we choose the best and most real".

A communist speaker at a rally, Nov. 1996:
"God is with us, comrades!"

Notes
[1] N.V. Gogol. Mertvye dushi, – in: N.V.Gogol, Sobranie khudozhestvennykh proizvedenii v pyati tomakh, tom V, s. 355-356. ("Dead Souls", excerpt translated into English by S.Plekhanov).
[2] Peter Reddaway and Dmitri Glinski, *The Tragedy of Russia's Reforms: Market Bolshevism Against Democracy* (Washington, DC: The United State Institute of Peace, 2001) 34. The expression was coined by Georgi Arbatov, Director of the Institute of USA and Canada, Russian Academy of Sciences, in a 1992 article published in the International Herald Tribune.
[3] Zernistye mysli nashikh politikov, vybrannye Konstantinom Dushenko, M. Eksmo- Press, 2002.

Cracking the Enigma Code: Russia's Usable Past

Professor Richard Pope, York University

The question has been asked: Can Russia Change? As we have seen in today's conference presentations, Russia has already changed amazingly and unimaginably, and it will continue to do so. How it will change is the question, and whether it will change for the better or worse.

There has always been great interest in this 'quo vadis' theme, especially among Russians themselves: a nation obsessed from earliest times with history and destiny and a sense of moving towards some great goal. But nobody knows where the famous troika is flying. Certainly in 1991 nobody predicted its course. Like Gogol's mad Poprishchin at the end of his 'Diary of a Madman', we all simply stood in wonder and gawked.

Let us leave aside what E.H. Carr calls "the teleological view of history" and all postulates of some "goal towards which the historical process is moving",[1] as well as any ideas that history is progressive or has discernible laws, behaving 'zakonomerno' with popularity.

Let us also grudgingly agree that history does not actually repeat itself, though at times it seems to, and that history does not teach any clear lessons that can be applied to the future. As Liudmila Jordanova points out, in *History in Practice*, it is simplistic to think "that unambiguous lessons from history exist, which provide simple formulae according to which present policies can and should be formulated".

How, then, can we profit from Russian history? What is Russia's 'usable past?' How should we approach Russia with an eye to the future?

Churchill famously described Soviet foreign policy as "a riddle wrapped in a mystery inside an enigma". Russia has been notoriously difficult for the West to understand. There is a sense, even among Russians, of Russia being special and ununderstandable. As the poet Tiutchev, put it, "the proud gaze of the foreigner will never understand Russia" (Ne poimet I ne zametit/ Gordyi vzor inoplemennyi).

Many special problems compound the difficulty: i.e, the problem of 'pokazukha' and the Potemkin village; a 1000-year tradition of Church and State censorship; and a startling tradition of falsification of history, as the opening of the Soviet archives is making only too clear. We are dealing with a state that has devoted enormous energy to hiding its true face from outsiders itself (i.e, the Inturist travel agency set up to keep foreigners from seeing the real Russia and Russia from seeing the rest of the world).

So, how can we crack the enigma code?

It is, of course, naïve to think we can predict how a people or a country will act, react, or change. But we can study how it has reacted in various situations in the past, examine the pressures that shaped those reactions, and then bear them in mind as possible parts of the equation when analyzing the present or trying to make educated guesses about the future.

Russia is currently fluid, volatile, vital, but it is not a 'tabularasa'. Where Russia is going will surely be influenced by where it has been. So, the question is not just where is Russia going, but where has she been? Where is Russia coming from?

Let us examine some of the constants that have been shaping forces affecting change in Russia's past, that may be affecting her present, and that could influence and/or shape Russia's unknowable future.

Factors that May Influence Russia's Future Course:

1. Consider the concept of 'smuta' – rebellion, agitation, disturbance, disorder, alarm, anxiety, the key ingredients of times of trouble ('smutnye vremena'). The Russian people have had a recurring confrontation with times of trouble beginning in the ninth century (862), when, as the oldest Russian chronicle, *The Tale of Bygone Years*, tells us, there was fratricidal strife and civil war as tribe rose against tribe.

The period, actually called the 'Times of Troubles', took place after the collapse of the Riurik dynasty. 1605-13 was a period of civil war, hunger, famine, cannibalism, brigandage, foreign intervention, murders, and pretenders. Dark forces were rampant.

The period after the collapse of the Romanov dynasty, 1917-21, was not all that different – civil war, chaos, madness, complete moral collapse, terror, bloody violence, population upheaval, refugees. There was an apocalyptic sense of Armageddon.

After the collapse of the Soviet dynasty, people took to the streets. So did tanks. At one point the White House, the Russian parliament building, was on fire. There was a breakdown of law and order – the hallmark of a time of trouble – corrupt police, rampant crime and corruption, collapse of the social net and the ruble, and people were confused about who had the power – the President or the local governors? Who were the oligarchs? Who controls the military? 'Kto kogo' (who will get whom)?

Should we have foreseen anything differently from what happened in Russia since 1991, with the exception that they avoided the kind of civil war that occured in the break-up of Yugoslavia? Should we have expected orderly change? Or can we see what happened as 'part of a continuum', a recurring pattern, a 'smuta': with the typical spread of the moods of pessimism, hopelessness, anger, and alarm as well as the corruption, the sense of chaos ad drift, and the collapse of rationality with the usual turn to faith healers, mysticism, astrology and the occult to fill spiritual void?

2. Because of their familiarity with 'smuta', the Russian people have a deep-seated fear of chaos and civil war above all. Perhaps the central theme of Russian literature and art, from the Igor Tale to Pelevin's *Chapaev i Pustota* is 'smuta' and the attempt to make sense out of it.

From Mongol times, this fear of chaos has been accompanied by a willingness to submit to a 'krepkity khoziain' – a strong boss. The condemnation of princely weakness and squabbling was already a theme in the eleventh-century *Life of Boris and Gleb*. The absolutist lesson of the Mongol Khan was not subsequently lost on the likes of Ivan III, Ivan IV, Peter I, Lenin, and Stalin. The enduring desire to feel "that someone above…is firmly in charge"[2] has been repeatedly exploited in the past.

Why might it not be exploited now in a period of insecurity, war, and social collapse? Democratic institutions in Russia have always been ill-fated: the 'veche', the 'boyar duma', the 'zemskii sobor', the 'Duma' of 1905. The Tartar model of absolutism has always had stronger resonance. Tsar' Boris Yelsin, as you may have noticed, had a tendency to impose democracy from the top down by 'ukaz'. Top-down imposition of market reform, 'Market Bolshevism', has been much in evidence since 1991.

Putin is no closet democrat. He likes to impose his will on the Russian people. He has surrounded himself almost exclusively with career bureaucrats, who owe their positions to patronage, rather than popular mandate. He is no friend of open media and free speech. His KGB background has shaped him. He recently had Stalin included among the war heroes in a Kremlin plaque. And yet he is popular because of his black belt, power skiing, and perceived strength. Here we see the Russian people's tendency to forgive excesses in exchange for order and hoped-for prosperity. It would be vain to predict it, but further moves in this direction, if they come, should come as no surprise.

3. Russia, like all absolutist states, has no history of respect for the law; no Magna Carta, no constitution, no laws that bound even the leader, no history of power-sharing, no empowering of the commons. The leader has always been above the law. Few would argue Putin is accountable now. Russian leaders have governed by 'ukaz', not 'zakon'. It is still difficult to get justice in Russian courts, especially if you are an environmentalist, foreign capitalist, or a relative of a Nord-Ost hostage crisis gassing victim.

But why should we expect respect for law and tolerance of dissent to appear overnight in Russia? Russia has always had a tradition of harsh repression of dissent: from Ivan and his 'oprichnina' to the 'Cheka' and the CPSU.

Putin's moves to suppress the media and free speech are hardly surprising from someone accustomed to an age-old tradition of harsh censorship. Even Gorbachev's famous 'glasnost' was limited, as Chernobyl made clear. Putin's slow strangling of the media and move towards a pre-glasnost position is almost to be expected.

4. The strength of Russian nationalism and the hallowing of tradition can hardly be over estimated. The belief in *Rus'* and the 'rodina' (native land) and the 'russkaia dusha' (Russian soul), the belief that Russia has the true faith, the idea that Russia is for Russians and the minorities should be Russified, the romantic/sentimental belief in the superiority of the 'narod' (the people) – these are all well-known parts of a potent myth. As we know, Stalin, who was not even a Russian, understood this well.

Is it surprising that Putin approved of resurrecting the music of the Soviet national anthem and the use of the Red flag by the Russian army (that he tolerates the Stalin cult) or that he wages war on Chechnya? Not if we believe that myth affects contemporary choices. And if it doesn't, just why did the Russians do such things as: rebuild the mighty cathedral, Khram Khrista- Spasitelya, exactly where and as it was before Stalin dynamited it; or go back to the name St. Petersburg and all the pre-Revolutionary street names; or restore the Throne Room in the Kremlin, as Yeltsin had Putin do? This can all be seen as more than a mere attempt to reconnect with the beneficial side of tradition. In Russia, the importance of traditions transcends the merely symbolic and instigates action.

The Russian president, for example, gambled on the Second Chechen War to divert hostility on the homefront in tough times, to awaken nationalism, foment patriotism, and to increase his popularity, just as Nicholas II did with the 'short victorious war' against Japan. Russia has a history of foreign adventurism in tough economic/political times.

Among other things, the powers that be counted on Russia's age-old hostility to 'others', her distrust of the alien, and fear of the strange. To the Russian peasant, everything outside his natal village was *chuzhoi* (strange, alien), even the next village was alien and to be feared. Hostility was expected from all who were different. Above all, foreigners were to be feared: the Khazars, the Polovtsians, the Mongols, the Germans, the Chinese, the Caucasian hillsmen. It is no surprise that so many Russians supported the Second Chechen War.

5. Should it surprise us that the anti-war movement in Russia is so small? Or that Russians are not out in the streets protesting against the

invasion of Iraq? Or that they are not at the polling booths in huge numbers?

Many Russians are cynical and of little faith that they can influence the course of events. There is no robust civil society yet. But then for centuries the gap between rulers and ruled was unspannable. 'Rus' and 'Rossiia' were contrasting cultural poles, at times coexisting in complete isolation one from the other with little in the middle. Is this not a cause of the current deep alienation among Russians?

In a memoir in 1994, Yeltsin claimed that he eliminated the 'seemingly endless gulf' between ordinary Russians and their government. Sadly he was wrong. Politicians can still get elected without building a constituency and enduring grilling by citizens and an aggressive press; there is little accountability. Civil rights can be eroded almost without protest. Citizens feel disempowered and that they have little control over change. Civil society is undermined by authoritarian tendency and the age-old gap between the leaders and the led. Anyone expecting the Russian people to quickly play a decisive role in directing Russia's future path will probably be disappointed. Civil disobedience, democracy, and accountability may come, but not quickly. Sergei Plekhanov feels that the role of the people in charge is inevitable: "It is hard to imagine the Russian people remaining in the role of passive onlookers and patient followers." I hope he is right and I am wrong.

One thinks of the Russian people's legendary silent obedience and passivity, the despair of the populist revolutionaries. The people's strong democratic values were a myth. Here, we have a people, for the better part of a millennium, isolated in the countryside, oppressed by the tyranny of work, poverty, and the influence of the village commune; a people whose religion stressed the redemptive value of suffering, non-resistance to evil, and acceptance of God's will; a people resistant to change, who placed great value on tradition and had a naïve belief in their leader as benevolent, but misinformed. Should we expect a robust civil society to emerge quickly among a people thus formed? Should it surprise us that according to most recent polls the people have little faith in elections and only a small minority support democracy?

6. When trying to fathom Russia's sometimes-belligerent foreign policy, should we not keep in mind Russia's age-old inferiority complex, her perceived need to explain her backwardness and lateness, and her abiding desire not to appear weak in any way? Now everyone knows that Russia cannot feed itself, the housing shortage is still acute, the living standard is low, crime is rampant, and the life expectancy is declining. Russia has been reduced to washing its dirty linen in public, something it rarely does. Humiliation and aggression often go hand in hand in life and in politics, particularly Russian politics, and should this not be borne in mind lest Western foreign policy needlessly drive Russia into a confrontational posture, as it has so often done in the past?

Conclusion

Should we not expect Russia to be influenced by historical cultural patterns that have affected here consistently throughout her past? I think that we in the West, particularly in North America with its mere three or four centuries of tradition, should be keenly aware of the power of myth and a millennium of cultural inertia to influence realpolitik, even if only to feign sympathetic insight into the difficulties Russia's leaders are facing.

This is the enigma to me: why are our expectations of Russia, both present and future, not more firmly based upon the usable past? The myths of Russian culture have shaped the "ideas and allegiances of Russian politics"[3] and foreign policy. There is no reason to think they will cease to do so. Russia's past is our main tool for understanding the present and possible directions in future.

Notes

[1] E.H Carr, *What is History?* (Harmondsworth, Middlesex: Penguin Books, 1965).

[2] Hedrick Smith, *The Russians*, (New York: Quadrangle/New York Times Book Co., 1976) 249.

[3] Orlando Figes, *Natasha's Dance: A Cultural History of Russia*, (New York: Henry Hold and Company, 2002) xxxi.

"Oumom Rossiyou nie poniat ..."

Professor Anne Leahy, Université du Québec à Montréal

"La raison ne saurait embrasser la Russie,
Elle ne se mesure pas à l'archine commune;
Elle est particulière –
En la Russie, on ne peut que croire."
                              Tioutchev (1803-1873)

Combien de fois ai-je entendu ces vers célèbres de Tioutchev au cours des années quatre-vingt-dix lorsque je vivais à Moscou! Le plus souvent, ils étaient évoqués par des étrangers qui cherchaient à y voir clair. On les entendait aussi chez les Russes, qui de leur côté cherchaient à faire comprendre leur pays. Ceux-ci se répartissaient, grosso modo, en réalistes, qui auraient voulu faire mentir Tioutchev en affirmant que « la Russie est un pays normal » et en fatalistes et nostalgiques. Ces derniers, au contraire, se consolaient auprès du poète à l'intuition que les Russes sont uniques.

Fiodor Ivanovich Tioutchev visait probablement avant tout ses propres compatriotes lorsqu'il composa ces vers qui saisissent assurément une part de vérité. Je crois que la popularité du président actuel de Russie, tout pragmatique qu'il soit, tient également à cette vérité. Il veut redonner à ses compatriotes des raisons de croire en la Russie. Plus qu'une simple transformation politique et économique, le défi de la métamorphose se situe à ce niveau.

Permettez-moi un mot sur Tioutchev. Il est bien sûr poète et écrivain; moins connu est le fait qu'il ait exercé le deuxième plus vieux métier du monde, la diplomatie. Il passa vingt-deux ans à Munich de 1822 à 1844 avant de rentrer au bercail au ministère des Affaires étrangères à St. Petersbourg. Il a publié plusieurs ouvrages qu'il vaut la peine de mentionner tant les préoccupations d'alors sont d'actualité un siècle et demi plus tard: "La Russie et l'Allemagne", "La Russie et la revolution", "La Russie et l'occident" et "La question de la papauté". Tioutchev s'avère donc un guide d'expérience pour nous qui examinons le "Défi de la métamorphose" de la Russie.

Métamorphose : plus que l'économique et le politique

Le thème de cette conférence a fait l'objet de nombreuses analyses, théories et déjà de relectures dans cette dernière décennie. Il est facile de regretter les laissés pour compte des réformes, trop vite ou pas assez vigoureusement poussées et de déplorer que les vieux démons de la corruption règnent en maître. Au fait, la Russie a-t-elle vraiment changé? Can Russia morph? pourrait-on se demander sur ce campus bilingue du Collège universitaire Glendon à Toronto.

Les appréciations de la décennie écoulée en Russie sont plus ou moins sévères selon sa conviction que les formules occidentales de représentation politique, d'implication de la société, du respect du droit et des lois du marché sont transférables à la Russie. La Russie a vécu après 1989 une période marquante de son histoire que certains n'hésitent pas à qualifier de révolution. C'était certainement au moins une période de "grand dérangement", pour reprendre une expression de notre histoire.

On a observé successivement des dislocations politiques, économiques et sociales, un vacuum au centre, une prise en main des leviers du pouvoir et éventuellement le recentrage en cours. Beaucoup a été dit sur les politiques suivies par le premier groupe de réformateurs autour du président Yeltsine, associé à Yégor Gaïdar. La plus grosse faillite de ces réformateurs, les néo-libéraux du style FMI, est d'avoir poursuivi une quête de réforme économique sans grand égard à la justice sociale, à la répartition équitable des ressources. Même à l'époque, la politique des privatisations, en particulier la grande braderie des ressources naturelles, était contestable et fut contestée mais peu.

La critique cinglante de Joseph Stiglitz, alors vice-président sénior et économiste en chef de la Banque mondiale et la réplique de Vladimir Mau, figure politique et économiste russe, résument à elles seules la désillusion des experts étrangers et la frustration des réformateurs russes (respectivement Whither Reform? Ten Years of the Transition, Washington, avril 1999 et Russian Economic Reforms as Perceived by Western Critics ("Anti-Stiglitz"), 1999). Cette polémique nous montre surtout qu'il n'y avait pas, ni pour les experts du FMI ni pour leurs interlocuteurs russes, de manuel d'emploi pour ces réformes (propos de Vladimir Mau repris par le président Poutine) et que les oligarches avaient le dessus au Kremlin où personne ne pouvait plus enrayer leur cupidité et celles de leurs partenaires. Ceci laisse la Russie aujourd'hui avec palmarès économique mixte: une grande réduction de l'endettement public mais un PIB encore 30% moindre qu'en 1990, un faible taux d'investissement et 40% de la population vivant sous le seuil de la pauvreté.

Il y a plus

Ayant vécu une partie de ces années à Moscou, je crois qu'il importe d'analyser le défi de la métamorphose en gardant bien à l'esprit le contexte de l'époque. Il faut se rappeler que la transformation ne se résume pas à la seule économie. Le comportement des russes, y compris suite à la crise du rouble en août 98 nous incite être tolérants dans nos analyses. Surtout, nous devons éviter, avec le recul, de porter un jugement plus sévère sur les événements tels qu'ils se déroulaient que celui que les Russes eux-mêmes ont porté à l'époque.

Le fait le plus marquant pour moi de la deuxième moitié des années 90 a été l'acquiescence de la population aux mouvements imprimés par les réformateurs de la première heure, et ce malgré les grandes difficultés matérielles qu'elle a endurées. Malgré les fraudes financières, pensons aux pyramides Mavrodi et à la "mère de toutes les pyramides" les certificats des Finances de 1998, malgré les manipulations électorales, et en dépit de l'impunité des oligarches, le message populaire exprimé aux dirigeants est demeuré constant – poursuivre la transformation du système. Et ce, même lorsque dès 1997, les mots « réformateur » et « démocrate » étaient devenus péjoratifs au point d'être évités par les « vrais » démocrates libéraux, conséquence directe de l'exploitation éhontée des ressources de l'état au profit de quelques favoris et au détriment de millions de gens.

Volonté de croire en la Russie

Une explication rationnelle ne suffit pas à comprendre cette volonté populaire et c'est là qu'intervient Tioutchev. La grande majorité des russes (ethniques et citoyens) où qu'ils se situent socialement et politiquement croient fondamentalement en leur patrie. Ils ont besoin d'y croire. Ce sentiment relève du sacré, un tout autre ordre que le politique qui a apporté son lot de tragédies aux russes au cours des siècles, si bien décrit par Hélène Carrère d'Encausse dans le "Le malheur russe".

Le Canadien pourtant familier de la quête d'identité nationale, ne peut qu'admirer la persistance des intellectuels russes à travers les âges à définir l'"idée russe". Le philosophe Berdiaiev, le contestataire Soljénitsyne, l'homme politique Yeltsine s'y sont essayés au vingtième siècle; le premier ministre Poutine s'y est attardé dans son message du millénaire. Les grands romanciers d'avant la révolution ont vécu, aidé à créer et dépeint un idéal de la vie russe. Même si elle se définit mal, la certitude d'une "russisté" est profondément ancrée chez le Russe et est la force qui lui permet justement de survivre aux traumatismes de son époque.

La gouvernance à besoin de confiance

Un des traits marquants de l'histoire récente de la Russie est ce moment de grâce du tout début des années quatre-vingt dix, lorsque la classe politique qui s'est portée au pouvoir a rejoint les aspirations de la majorité des russes. Des hommes politiques, Sakharov, Yeltsine étaient portés par la confiance des Russes. Ce n'était plus l'"avenir radieux" des communistes. Il était plausible d'espérer en des jours meilleurs. Pour un instant, on a cru possible de faire avancer la chose publique et instaurer une ère de légitimité du pouvoir fondé sur la confiance, élément indispensable de la gouvernance.

On connaît la suite. La nécessité des réformes était acceptée mais les comportements excessifs (le "bespredel") des barons économiques et d'une certaine classe politique ont bientôt miné la confiance des gens dans la volonté des élus à protéger leurs intérêts. Déjà en 1996, cette belle période de1990 à 1993 (jusqu'à l'assaut de la Maison-blanche) fut qualifiée, et sans regret, de "romantique".

Après la crise d'août 1998, la Douma a forcé le président Yeltsine à nommer Yevguenii Primakov, dont l'expérience remontait à l'époque soviétique, comme Premier ministre. Il est vite devenu l'homme politique le plus populaire (s'assurant ainsi malheureusement un bref mandat) entre autres parce qu'il s'est attaqué ouvertement à un certain oligarche. On lui prêta des intentions de retour à l'arrière, ce qui ne fut pas le cas. Des experts néo-libéraux de leur côté, poussaient fort le modèle économique argentin et son « currency board » et firent venir le ministre Carvalho pour expliquer aux autorités ses effets en apparence salutaires. Heureusement, le modèle qui semblait si efficace à l'époque ne fut pas adopté.

Pendant son mandat, le Premier ministre Primakov disait qu'aucun gouvernement ne ferait avancer son programme s'il ne bâtissait pas une relation de confiance avec les citoyens. Autrefois, personne ne faisait confiance aux communistes et voilà que l'impuissance du gouvernement à contrôler les débordements des oligarches et potentats régionaux menait à la même incapacité politique.

La clé dans tout cela n'est pas une réforme de plus ou de moins mais la relation que les politiciens au pouvoir entretiennent avec la population. Cyniquement, on peut dire qu'elle n'a jamais été un facteur dans l'histoire de la Russie mais ce ne serait pas tout à fait vrai et ce l'est de moins en moins. Les moyens de résistance passive ont toujours existé : ils font semblant de nous payer, nous faisons semblant de travailler; pas de services sociaux, pas d'impôts. Aujourd'hui, il faut compter en plus avec les associations de défense de droits de toutes sortes qui varient énormément en efficacité mais qui sont présentes.

C'est la recherche d'un équilibre entre deux facteurs qui permet de gouverner la Russie sur la voie de l'ouverture : le pouvoir doit manifester qu'il contrôle les leviers – l'étatisme sera toujours nécessaire et le pouvoir doit apprendre à tolérer l'expression des droits et libertés de sa population même si cela peut signifier une alternance au pouvoir. Ceci n'est pas encore fait. Et c'est là qu'est notre dilemme car je crois qu'en Russie, la force de l'état et le respect de la nation dans le monde primeront sur toute autre considération. C'est un peu ce que nous dit Tioutchev.

A Cyclical Theory of Russia's Historical Change

Professor Georgi M. Derluguian, Northwestern University

An observer situated in 1950 (or in 1960, 1970, and still in 1985) would have seen Russia and the Caucasus as completely different from what was there before 1917. The political and ideological structures have changed substantially, to say the least; the social configurations have changed almost beyond recognition; and the landscape itself has undergone the transformation from a mostly agrarian and rural to being predominantly urban and industrial. In short, the period between 1917 and 1945 would appear marked by overwhelming discontinuities.

By contrast, our contemporary observer from the 1990s and the 2000s might see striking continuities with the epochs before the revolution of 1917 if not before the completion of Russian territorial conquests in the 1860s-1870s. Some commentators even argue that nothing ever changes. On the surface, this is not an entirely false impression. Back is the imperial double-headed eagle instead of hammer and sickle; the Russian armies are once again trying to subdue Chechnya; a former superpower looks impoverished and backward. And like the last tsars a century earlier, the new rulers face the intractable dilemma of reforms that are opposed by the vested interests of self-serving bureaucracies and a small but powerful oligarchic class who at the same time remain as the pillars of the ruling regime. It looks like the whole twentieth century was a big, bloody waste.

What we observe, however, is not the re-emergence of primordial cultural bedrock after the interlude of presumably deviant communist efforts to change history and human nature itself. It is another historical phase when Russia is again moving downward in the world hierarchy of power and wealth, toward a more peripheral position in relation to the leading capitalist sectors of the West. And this is not for the first time.

From the outset the Russian and other East European feudalisms were more rudimentary than the analogous social patterns in the medieval West. The reasons for the disparity were structural. The eastern side of Europe lacked the rich deposits of Roman inheritance (towns, roads, etc.) At the same time, unlike the western side sheltered by the Alps and the band of thick forests running in the middle of Europe, the eastern side was geopolitically exposed to the pressure of predatory nomadic cavalries from the Eurasian Steppe.[1]

This situation was reversed in the 1480s-1550s after the Muscovite grand princes (the ancestors of Tsar Ivan the Terrible and especially the young Ivan himself) succeeded in building an adequately strong and centralized patrimonial state. The state-building process required the cunning and cruelty that generally characterized Renaissance politics. But the particular reliance of Russian state-builders on coercion was neither idiosyncratic nor pre-ordained by the notorious cultural 'legacies of Chingiz-khan'. The coercion, as Tilly persuasively argues, was not so much a willful choice of early state-builders as it was the strategy. Its main reason and advantage was to compensate for the relative scarcity of capitalist resources within a thinly populated realm like Russia, which was also true of imperial Spain and Prussia.[2]

The emergent Muscovite kingdom was a great success within its historical class, as judged by its ability to develop the production of firearms, create the new service nobility and a standing army, and subsequently to push its frontiers far eastward, eliminating in the process the Tatar khanates of Volga and Siberia. Another measure of state-building success is the divergent trajectories of early modern Russia and another large and arguably very coercive realm in Eastern Europe, Poland-Lithuania. Where the Polish aristocratic confederation de-industrialized, de-urbanized, and eventually disappeared from the map (all despite the Poles' much asserted cultural belonging to the West), the less Western but despotically centralized Russia eventually could join the European world-system on honorable terms as one of the most powerful states of its time.[3]

This second historical achievement of the Russian state came at the price of further coercion. Towards the seventeenth century Muscovy once again lagged behind in the creation of an absolutist state that represented the most advanced technique of power in its epoch. Catching up with European absolutism took the vigorous and unabashedly ruthless reforms of Tsar Peter in the early 1700s carried on by the enlightened despotism of Catherine the Great in the 1760s-1790s. The absolutist cycle of Russia culminated in the early nineteenth century with the defeat of Napoleon, and the brief occupation of Paris, and the acquisition of vast territories from Poland to Ottoman Turkey, Persia, and all the way to the frontiers of imperial China.

The Russian absolutist achievement followed the coercion-intensive path that might look different from the mainly capital-intensive path of the Western core states, though not as entirely different as the normative-juridical presentations of modern history would make us believe. In the analytical scheme of capital- and coercion-intensive paths of modern state building, Russia gravitated toward the coercion end of the distribution but still remained perfectly within the scope of contemporary state 'physiologies'.[4]

The scarcity of capitalist resources remained a durable and self-reproducing constraint. The rulers of Russia, generation after generation, had to concern themselves with what elsewhere in the core states of the world system was one of the chief functions of the capitalist pursuit of profit: the creation and ongoing modernization of production bases. To stress the key difference, perhaps at the expense of overgeneralization: if in the Western core states the secular trend was the bureaucratic rationalization of capitalism plus state coercion, in Russia it was the bureaucratic rationalization of state coercion minus capitalism. This morphological difference marks the non-belonging of Russia to the core of the capitalist world-economy. Russia has always been only a semi-peripheral state though at times an inordinately important state, even a super-power. This also renders Russia one of the earliest and longest-running developmental states in history that has been 'developing', i.e. catching up with the capitalist core, for nearly five hundred years.

At the historical peaks achieved in the ascending phases of coercion-intensive developmental reforms, the Russian state almost caught up and moved closer to the threshold of the world-system's core. Military and productive parity was achieved several times in Russia's history. But the state's mobility always stopped there. The disruptive and traumatic changes seemed no longer necessary because Russia has already entered the comfortable plateaus of geopolitical power-prestige in relation to the West. Such plateau phases eventually created the impression of the internal 'ossification' of Russia as the leading elites of each successful period would stabilize socially, entrench themselves politically, and begin reaping the fruits of their hard-won position. In the meantime, the West would discover yet another more advanced technique of rule: absolutism, industrial imperialism, welfare state, or neoliberal globalization. The plateau phases of relative parity ended, and once again Russia looked as though it was lagging behind by the contemporary core standards, though not necessarily weaker compared to its own achievements in previous epochs – in the seventeenth century Muscovy still was a major power in its neighbourhood; in the late nineteenth century the Russian Empire was far better off than Turkey,

Persia, or China; in the 1970s the USSR enjoyed the highest-ever levels of internal consumption in Soviet history and remained a nuclear superpower feared and respected by Washington. Yet the growing gap between the aspirations of the Russian state and its diminishing capabilities in the evolving world-system, i.e. the renewed relative backwardness, haunted the rulers of Russia.

Even more so, the perceptions of shameful disparity with the West troubled the growing number of domestic critics and would provide them a basis for their criticism. Such critics and their potential constituencies themselves emerged as the result of previous developmental efforts. In the ascendant phases, the Russian reformist rulers fostered the education of technical specialists and, for the prestigious and ideological purposes of state, they also cultivated artists, thinkers, and scholars who could imitate and eventually counter the contemporary Western achievements in analogous fields. The cultural-symbolic and expert-technical aspects of the reforms opened new social fields and careers that, in turn, attracted active and inventive applicants much in excess of what the state ever wanted or could manage. In the phases of stabilization, plateau, decline, and crisis the state found itself increasingly lacking the means to incorporate and control its mid-ranking specialists and the intellectuals who were turning into domestic critics.

A prototype of this social mechanism is found already in the church schism and the tremendous popular movement of radical 'Old believers' ('starovery') in the seventeenth century. It was made possible by the state centralization of the ecclesiastical field during the previous epoch that resulted in the creation of structural tensions and resources for the Russian Orthodox version of Reformation and Counter-reformation. In the late imperial and again in the late Soviet periods, the state developmental reforms gave rise to secular intelligentsias, the famed sub-elite groups who held the key cultural capitals of their epochs. Eventually the intelligentsia began using their position to formulate a strong moral condemnation of the ruling classes and the state. As the fissures in the dominant bloc grew apparent and different elite factions sought allies outside their circle if not an outright opportunity to defect, the intelligentsia's moral condemnation gained the opportunity to escalate into open political opposition. At least some symbolic capitals of the intelligentsia then could be converted into political and later the administrative capital, which is probably how Pierre Bourdieu would have described a Russian revolutionary sequence.

Theda Skocpol is certainly right in detecting the causal links between triggering events such as war defeat forcing the escalation of elite factionalism and thus opening the way for social revolution.[5] Lenin and Trotsky knew it just as well, but their formulations served rather the purposes of non-academic revolutionary theory that they were finally able to test in practice. Already the revolution from above waged by Peter the Great was in direct response to the earlier signalling defeats at the hands of the Turks, the Crimean Tatars, and the Swedes. The revolution of 1905 followed the acute humiliation from the Japanese navy that was previously considered a laughable proposition. By the beginning of 1917 the imperial apparatus proved patently unable to withstand the combined pressures of German offensive and internal dissent arising from all sectors of society. At the beginning of Gorbachev's reforms in 1985, however, neither the military situation in Afghanistan nor at the static Cold War fronts against the NATO and China seemed immediately threatening by a possible defeat. Nonetheless with all available evidence the contemporary Soviet leadership felt hard pressed to act before the situation deteriorated beyond repair (i.e. not unlike the young tsar Peter), which indicated the importance and perhaps even the relative autonomy of the symbolic and ideological level of causality.

Next in order would be the incorporation into our theory of geopolitical regularities empirically detected and theorized in a Weberian vein by Randall Collins.[6] The spatial size of the Russian state has been growing over its entire history until 1991. (A popular impressionistic estimate gives the average rate of five square kilometres a day – over nearly five centuries). The territorial expansion inevitably transformed Russia from its originally marchland position into a central power, which also happened several times, apace with the expansion of the systems of military strategic relations in which Russia found itself. The alternation of marchland and central power geopolitical positioning of Russia forms a cycle of its own. But here we might need to introduce additional mechanisms in order to explain why Russia has been able to escape the geopolitical traps. In this, we could draw on Tilly's theorizing of state-building and on the world-systems analysis, especially Arrighi's conceptualization of territorial accumulation as, up to a point, a viable alternative to capitalism.[7]

Russia has been overcoming the geopolitical constraint by the combination of quantitative expansion of its territorial and natural resources base and the qualitative bursts of modernizing reforms. It fostered the military and tax-extractive capabilities that matched or exceeded the capabilities of Russia's geopolitical rivals. This pattern began in the late medieval period when the principality of Moscow first transformed itself from a second-rate political unit into the forceful unifier and centralizer of Russian lands. The combined resources were then used to build the gunpowder empire and internalize the Steppe frontier. Peter, followed by Catherine, forced their way into the geopolitics of Europe not only by wrestling control over the Baltic from the Swedes but mainly by vastly expanding the productive and demographic bases in the eastern and southern reaches of their fast growing empire. No Western state at the time could match it. And lastly, the towering achievement of the Soviet mobilizational economy was to end the geopolitical exceptionalism of the United States by mass-producing nuclear weapons and the rocket means of delivery. Collins's geopolitical theory provides a powerful explanatory tool in the first approximation. It must be expanded and combined with other theories in order to clarify how the geopolitical regularities mesh with the internal dynamics of state transformations and the flow of resources at the levels of geoculture and world-economy. This goal seems achievable in the near future.[8]

Finally, we shall need to move forward in developing the state-centered theory of revolutions from the foundations laid by Skocpol, Tilly, and their collaborators. They have accomplished a lot. To begin with, these scholars achieved the seminal shift away from the canonical nineteenth-century views of revolutions as either the popular liberating events (or horrifying eruptions of base 'crowd' instincts) which summarizes the typical feelings of participants, or, in a more abstract generalization, the necessary rapid transitions between historical stages, as commonly held by the traditional Liberal idea of 'bourgeois' revolution and its Marxist counterpart. Revolutions are now seen as predominantly the instances of state breakdown. Whatever causes it, the breakdown opens the hitherto unavailable possibilities to perform a wholesale restructuring of the state, that may (or may not, or may for the time being) solve its previously intractable problems. Put differently, revolution begins with the sudden collapse that, if successfully exploited by a concerted political force, can result in a radical upgrading of state powers. This forms the full sequence that was traditionally singled out as the great or, in Skocpol's terms, social revolutions. Such full sequences culminating in a successful recomposition of the invigorated state are very rare in history. Obviously, a lot can go awry in the chaos of revolutions resulting instead in a half-way conservative restoration, protracted stagnation, even the disappearance of the state. Post-Soviet Russia is an example.

Revolutions viewed from the vantage point of state power clearly look akin to big reforms. (A Russian satire from 1905 nicely captured this connection by portraying the terrorist wing of Social Revolutionaries as 'liberals with bombs'). Tilly should be credited for drawing the analytical continuum that overcame the exceedingly ideological perception of revolutions as being an entirely separate species from the rebellions, revolutions-from-above, reforms, and simply collapses.[9]

But why have revolutions happened at all in the modern times? What did they really achieve? If they are not the direct result of liberation struggles waged by the downtrodden, and if at the end freedom is not what they gain, then what are they or what do they do? Another theoretical breakthrough of Theda Skocpol was to overcome the traditionally internalist analysis of revolutions and demonstrate instead the salience of external factors that she reduced to military defeat. Even if we add further down the sequence the revolutionary revanchiste conquests exemplified by Napoleon or Lenin and Stalin or in a latest example, Fidel Castro in Angola, this still does not solve the problem. We turn for help to Immanuel Wallerstein who does not merely bring the external factors into the analysis of revolutions but rather situates the revolutions and their outcomes in the plane of the modern world-system.[10]

Observed from this perspective, the modern revolutions have a lot to do with the mobility of states in the geopolitical hierarchy and the axial division of labor in the world-system. In simple terms, revolutions have been at the radical extreme of the more usual reform efforts intended to resist the downward decline of one's group position (country or nation) in the world's ranking order. The decline and backwardness, or their perceived effects on social, economic, and cultural fields, would be countered by restructuring the state and social composition of national society. In the countries outside the Western core, the liberal national reformers (who sometimes were as revolutionary as, for example, Atatürk) normally adhered to the Hegelian or Durkheimian ideas of historical progress and order. Their hope was that the state could foster the middle class because the rise of the latter is the explanation for European modernity and 'civic culture'. The Marxist-inspired revolutionaries rather saw the answer in the state-creation of industrial proletariat because their ideology associated an industrial proletariat with modernity and universal salvation.[11] Of course, these are quite different programs. What they had in common, however, was the view of the state as the key to catching up.

The main distinction was in the political means. Revolutions differ from reforms not in what they achieve – the strengthening of state structures to direct the socioeconomic and military changes.[12] The difference is really in how the modern revolutionary contenders proceeded to achieve these goals: by mobilizing the masses to destroy the old political and social order that they blamed for causing the decline and perpetuating backwardness. The Russian revolutions represent the dramatic destructive-constructive routes toward the transformation of first the state and then, the society. They were the moments when the dam burst, opening way to new streams that occurred in the situations when old regimes failed to overcome themselves. In Russia such bursts happened twice during the twentieth century: first, after 1917, and again in 1989-1992. The results were obviously different.

Generally, the successive modernizing leaps of the Russian state required the obliteration of social structures and the associated classes that, ironically, once served as the basis of the previous leap. Each time the transformation amounted to a revolution waged whether from above, by the monarchical reformers, or else – not entirely from below but rather by the contenders emerging from the middle-ranks of pre-revolutionary society who sought to channel the energies of the revolts from below. Ivan the Terrible murderously eliminated the decentralized feudal patterns. Peter the Great massacred the old guard of 'streltsy', created from scratch the new army, subordinated the church to secular bureaucracy, expanded by nearly ten-fold the ranks of service nobility, and built on a swamp, the new oceanic capital of St. Petersburg in order to leave behind the stalwarts of old order in the landlocked Moscow. Yet the last two tsars who assumed the reigns in the late nineteenth century could no longer risk radical reforms without provoking a revolution and alienating their shrinking social base – mainly the conservative and myopic nobility of ranking bureaucrats, military generals, and landowners whose ancestors a century earlier provided the dynamism and force to the absolutist reforms of Peter and Catherine. When in 1881 the revolutionary terrorists assassinated the reformer Alexander II, although his death was shocking, it was widely perceived by the ruling elite as the tsar's own fault. Thirty years later, the elite reaction to the killing of Prime-Minister Stolypin, the last reformer of the Old Regime, was nearly identical. Ultimately, the logjam created by Russia's Old Regime on the road to industrialization was eliminated in the revolution of 1917 and the Russian Civil war.

In the last decade the most recent attempt to reform and revolutionize the Soviet and then the Russian state foundered in the counter-rebellion of the communist nomenklatura who essentially took the state apart and privatized its most valuable assets. The unfinished business of reform or revolutionary transformation left the post-Soviet Russia at a nadir where it languishes now and threatens to slide further down to the periphery. It remains to be seen whether the structural trends of Russian state history can continue to operate in a world-system where the global trend of recent decades has been toward decreasing the salience of states. Yet the re-centralizing authoritarianism of Colonel Putin indicates that the same mechanisms are still running. It remains to be seen whether Putin or someone else will be able to batter the bailiwicks carved by the new-old oligarchy, repossess the looted state assets, and catch up with the core once again.

Notes

[1] Perry Anderson, *Passages from Antiquity to Feudalism*, (London: New Left Books, 1974) 213-244.

[2] Charles Tilly, *Coercion, Capital, and European States, AD 990 –1992*, (Oxford: Blackwell, 1992) 137-143; also see the discussion of state-formation, economic geography, and towns in Europe by Stein Rokkan, *State Formation, Nation-Building, and Mass Politics in Europe: The Theory of Stein Rokkan Based on His Collected Works*, edited by Peter Flora with Stein Kuhnle and Derek Urwin (Oxford: Oxford U. Press, 1999).

[3] Immanuel Wallerstein, *The Modern World-System*, Vol. I: *Capitalist Agriculture and the Origins of the European World-Economy in the Sixteenth Century*. (New York: Academic Press, 1974).

[4] See the outline of 'state physiologies' by Charles Tilly, *Coercion, Capital, and European States, AD 990 –1992*, (Oxford: Blackwell, 1992) 54-58. Another important discussion of 'territorialist versus capitalist modes of accumulation' is provided by Giovanni Arrighi, *The Long Twentieth Century: Money, Power, and the Making of Our Times*, (London: Verso, 1994). Arrighi's typology is historically and analytically broader than Tilly's, but the relative theoretical merits of the two conceptualizations are yet to be explored.

[5] Theda Skocpol, *States and Social* Revolutions, (Cambridge: Cambridge U. Press, 1979).

[6] Randall Collins, "The Geopolitical Basis of Revolution: The Prediction of the Soviet Collapse", in: idem, *Macrohistory,* (Stanford, 1999) 37-69.

[7] Charles Tilly, *Coercion, Capital, and European States, AD 990 –1992*. (Oxford: Blackwell, 1992); Giovanni Arrighi, *The Long Twentieth Century*. (London: Verso, 1994).

[8] See Randall Collins and David Waller, "Predictions of Geopolitical Theory and the Modern World-System," in: Georgi Derluguian and Scott L. Greer, eds, *Questioning Geopolitics*, (Westport: Praeger, 2000) 51-66.

[9] Charles Tilly, *European Revolutions, 1492-1992* (Oxford: Blackwell, 1993).

[10] See Immanuel Wallerstein, "The French Revolution as a World-Historical Event," in *Unthinking Social Science*, (Cambridge: Polity Press, 1991) 7-22; a detailed discussion of the French and Haitian revolutions and 'the settler decolonization of the Americas' is found in Immanuel Wallerstein, *The Modern*

World-System, Vol. 3 *Second Era of Great Expansion of the Capitalist World-Economy*. (San Diego: Academic Press, 1989).

[11] Bruce Cumings, "Webs with No Spiders, Spiders with No Webs: The Genealogy of the Developmental State," in: Meredith Woo-Cumings, ed, *The Developmental State* (Ithaca: Cornell U. Press, 1999) 70-71.

[12] The ambitious revolutionary claims to change the whole world always remained an ideological imagery and not the actual political practice, though perhaps at a grander plane it was a world-changing imagery. See Immanuel Wallerstein, *Utopistics*. (New York: The New Press, 1998).

Section 2

Political and Economic Challenges

Elections and Democracy in Russia[1]

Professor Joan DeBardeleben, Carleton University

Elections are one instrument of democracy, but political scientists disagree about whether free competitive elections themselves are adequate to warrant classifying a country as a democracy. In attempting to assess Russia's progress with democratization, understanding the role and importance of elections in this process is an important question.

Analysts have suggested several criteria by which to judge whether democracy has been 'firmed up' or consolidated. One is whether elections are 'the only game in town' to determine transfer of political power.[2] In other words, do political actors acknowledge their legitimacy and reject other extra-legal methods for gaining power. Also do political actors accept uncertain outcomes as the legitimate nature of democratic politics? By both of these criteria, Russia seems to qualify as a legitimate democratic system; even opposition parties seem to accept the necessity of working within the system and have not appealed to extra-legal measures when they have lost elections or been excluded from real political power following elections.

By another criterion, whether there has been a real turnover in power through the electoral process,[3] Russia does not meet the criterion of being a 'consolidated' democracy. This suggests that the process of democratization could still be reversed, or that it is still on possibly shaky ground. When Boris Yeltsin resigned as President, power was turned over to a 'designated successor' who was subsequently confirmed in office through a popular election. Vladimir Putin did not represent the political opposition, and it is still unclear whether all political forces would accept a transferrance of political power to the Communists if an election outcome went in this direction.

By yet another measure, whether elections have brought change in government or in policies, Russia again scores weakly. Despite the fact that the Communist Party of the Russian Federation got the largest number of votes in the 1995 and 1999 Duma elections, no change in government or prime minister followed. Elections in Russia have also been inefficacious in setting a mandate for new government and have been only weak vehicles of accountability. It is hard for citizens to know how to call their government to account, given the current structure of the political system. Elections have had, at best, an indirect effect on policy. Part of the reason lies in the weakness of Russian political parties as vehicles of governance and the continuing importance of patron-client relationship and personalism in Russian political life.

What do Russian themselves think about the state of Russian democracy and the role of elections in it? Survey data shows that while support for democratic values is relatively high by several measures, Russians are not satisfied with the way democracy works in their country. Elections themselves are apparently not viewed as effective instruments of democracy. This raises the question of 'why'. Prima facie, citizen dissatisfaction may suggest underlying inadequacies. Of course this dissatisfaction may also be rooted in inflated expectations or an unclear vision as to the proper role of elections. Following examination of the nature of this dissatisfaction, we draw some preliminary conclusions about obstacles to elections acting as effective vehicles of democracy in Russia. We should note at the outset that the analysis developed here relates exclusively to the national level and does not explore electoral arrangements or visions in the regions.

Citizen Views

Many surveys of public opinion have explored aspects of voter opinion or have sought to explain voting behaviour in Russia.[4] Other analysts have examined support for democratic values and democratic institutions.[5] Studies generally show fairly high levels of popular support for democratic values in Russia, although findings are more mixed when particular dimensions of democratic culture are examined. At the same time it is clear that many Russians are quite dissatisfied with the way democracy is actually practiced in Russia. Opinion surveys carried by Carleton University in conjunction with Russian partners provide a picture of this ambivalence about Russian democracy.

A problem faced by researchers is to determine what respondents understand the word 'democracy' to mean. Democracy is a particularly contested term in Russia, so it is necessary to try to understand how respondents understand the term before soliciting their assessments. So as not to assume a particular understanding of democracy among our Russian respondents, we gave them the opportunity to define democracy for themselves, through two vehicles. One was an open-ended question, "What comes to mind when you hear the word 'democracy' in Russia today?" A second measure was a close-ended question that asked respondents to relate particular institutional features to their understanding of the word. Answers reveal that Russians are quite cynical about democracy in practice but at the same time see democracy as embodying many features commonly associated with the term in liberal democratic countries of the West. As Table 1 reveals, almost 60% of Russian respondents have negative associations with the word democracy and many of these suggest ineffective governance involving features such as confusion, anarchy, distortion, lawlessness, criminality, and demagoguery.

Table 1: What comes to mind when you hear the word 'democracy' in Russia today?

	Russia 1995/1996	Russia 2000
General Positive Associations	**7.1**	**6.1**
Freedom	4.0	3.9
What We Are as a Country		
Positive Political/Legal Associations	**11.7**	**14.2**
Freedom of Speech, Press	5.0	5.9
Free Elections, Parties, Participation	2.3	0.7
Freedom of Religion, Conscience	2.0	2.0
Rule of Law, Equal Rights		
Government		
Positive Socio-Economic Associations	**0.8**	**0.6**
Market Economy, Prosperity		0.4
TOTAL POSITIVE ASSOCIATIONS	**19.6**	**20.9**
General Negative Associations	**30.9**	
Confusion, Chaos, Disintegration, Anarchy	16.7	11.9
Absence or Lack of Democracy	5.4	7.1
Mockery, Distortion	3.9	6.2
Negative Political/Legal Associations	**23.9**	**21.4**
Lawlessness	6.2	6.6
Criminality, Corruption, Dishonesty	4.1	6.6
Demagogues, Dictatorship, Control From the Top	3.5	2.9
Negative Socio-Economic Associations	**3.3**	**3.6**
Poverty, Inflation, Unemployment		1.5
Inequality, Unfairness		
TOTAL NEGATIVE REFERENCES	**58.1**	**57.1**
Other	**6.0**	**3.9**
Nothing, Don't Know, No Answer	**27.8**	**28.4**
Sample Size	**2080**	**2409**

*Analysis of the 1995 data is from Jon Pammett, "Elections and Democracy in Russia," *Communist and Post-Communist Studies*, 32 (1999), p.47 based on a Carleton 1995 Post-Election Survey. The survey involved a representative sample collected in 19 regions of Russia. The 2000 survey is from the Carleton University Regions, based on a representative sample in four regions of Russia.

Although levels of confidence in the honesty of elections are increasing, in 2000 almost half of respondents were still unconvinced about the integrity of electoral processes.

Table 2: Belief that Elections Were Carried Out Honestly in Russia* % of all Respondents

	1995 Duma	1996 Pres (1998	Most recent gubernatorial (1998 survey)	Most recent gubernatorial (2000 survey)	2000 Pres (2000 survey)
Yes &/or Definitely	11.5	11.9	23.8	24.6	28.5
Probably	26.9	19.0	26.6	25.8	27.4
Probably Not	23.2	20.0	10.5	10.5	12.5
Definitely Not	25.4	30.3	14.2	13.7	17.7
No Answer &/or Hard to Say	13.0	19.8	30.0	25.4	16.9
No	1902	1931	1931	2410	2410

*1995 data are based on a Carleton 1995 Post-Election Survey that involved a representative sample collected in 19 regions of Russia. The 1998 and 2000 are from the Carleton University Regions 1998 survey and the Carleton University Regions 2000 survey based on a representative sample in four regions of Russia (five in 1998, including,Yamal-Nenets Autonomous Okrug).

Russians show rising and quite high levels of trust in particular elected officials who were identified by name (Table 3), but positive feelings for elected institutions are much lower (Table 4), suggesting a personalistic basis for political support.

Table 3: Trust in Political Leaders At Various Levels of Government % that express trust or more trust than distrust

	President 1998	President 2000	State Duma Deputy 2000	Governor 2000	Governor 1998
Orlov oblast	7 (1)	84 (50)	66 (35)	87 (49)	88 (41)
Stavropol krai	24 (10)	89 (59)	60 (21)	65 (32)	78 (40)
Nizhegorodsk aia oblast	35 (7)	84 (50)	51 (16)	62 (23)	73 (21)
Khanty-Mansiisk	31(5)	90 (57)	74 (24)	95 (63)	71 (19)

* ('trust fully' in parentheses)
* Selected Russian Regions, 1998
* Data excludes those not answering or those indicating 'hard to say'.

Table 4: Thermometer Score for Elected Institutions and Elected Officials in Russia

	Putin	Governor (Named)	State Duma (Federal)	Regional Legislature
Orlov oblast	6.87	7.38	3.65	4.42
Stavropol krai	7.80	5.01	3.76	4.19
Nizhegorodskaia oblast	7.04	4.37	3.88	3.65
Khanty-Mansiisk A.O	7.63	7.59	4.16	6.40
Total	7.33	6.11	3.86	4.68

* The question asked respondent to rate each individual or institution on a scale of 1-10 where 1 is 'cold' and 10 is 'warm', in 2000.

When asked about general satisfaction with the level of democracy in Russia, about three-quarters of those answering expressed dissatisfaction.

Table 5: Levels of Satisfaction With Democracy in Russia

	Russia 1995	Russia 1998	Russia 2000
Satisfied	1.8%	1.6%	3.5%
More Satisfied Than Not	8.8	6.4	11.5
More Dissatisfied	38.5	37.1	34.9
Dissatisfied	50.9	54.9	50.1
Total N Responding	1659	1685	2165

* % of those responding, column percentages
*1995 data are based on a Carleton 1995 Post-Election Survey that involved a representative sample collected in 19 regions of Russia. The 1998 and 2000 are from the Carleton University Regions 1998 survey and the Carleton University Regions 2000 survey based on a representative sample in four regions of Russia (five in 1998, includingYamal-Nenets Autonomous Okrug).

In contrast to negative assessments of the current state of Russian democracy, the vast majority of Russian respondents express support for the idea of democracy and the adoption of a democratic model in Russia.

. **Table 6:** Support for Introduction of Democracy in Russia

	Yes, Definitely			More Yes than No		
	1995	1998	2000	1995	1998	2000
Orel	42.1	32.5	25.5	31.7	35.0	43.5
Stavropol	35.6	30.4	36.5	24.7	37.7	33.3
Nizhnii Novgorod	41.0	34.3	47.2	44.4	42.9	33.5
Khan-Man Okrug	49.4*	46.2	36.1	36.7	40.2	40.2
	More No than Yes			Definitely Not		
	1995	1998	2000	1995	1998	2000
Orel	14.6	18.5	18.0	11.6	14.0	13.0
Stavropol	22.6	13.2	16.9	17.1	18.7	13.3
Nizhnii Novgorod	8.3	13.0	11.1	6.3	9.8	8.8
Khan-Man Okrug	9.0	8.0	13.7	4.8	5.5	10.0

* Selected Russian Regions – 1995/96,1998, 2000
* Row percentages
* 1995 values are for a survey carried out in Khanty-Mansiisk and Yamal-Nenets Okrugs

But what vision of democracy are they inclined to embrace? Other questions in the survey help to clarify this question. While many Western studies identify 'liberty' as the key association with democracy in post-communist Eastern Europe, in our study we explored institutional correlates of Russians' democratic vision, with one of our measures directly focusing on the role of elections. We asked our respondents to rate the importance of a number of institutional features for their understanding of the true meaning of democracy. Comparisons between Russian responses (which are remarkably consistent over time) with data from a Canadian survey carried out in the year 2001 reveal some intriguing contrasts (Table 7).

Table 7: How Important Is Each of the Following to the Idea of Democracy?

	Russia 1998	Russia 2000	Canada 2001
Written Functioning Constitution	78	78	68
Independent Courts	72	72	52
Freedom of the Press	69	69	69
Right to Private Property	50	56	75
Regular Competitive Election	52	50	60
Assemblies at Which Citizens Make Decisions	50	49	43
Referenda on Important Questions	44	44	44
Competing Political Parties	31	32	58
Division of Power Between the Centre and Regions		26	

* (% saying very important or very essential)
* The 1998 data if from the 1998 Carleton University Regions survey and the 2000 data is from the Carleton University Regions 2000, survey based on a representative sample in five and four regions of Russia, respectively. The Canadian data is from the Kroeger College (Carleton)/Polaris 2001 survey. Thanks to Jon Pammett for access to this data.

Russians seem less convinced than Canadians about the importance of competitive elections and competing political parties, and more persuaded about the importance of 'rule of law' features such as an effective constitution, an independent judiciary and freedom of speech. While the latter may not be surprising as a reaction to the sometimes arbitrary nature of party/state power in the communist period, the lesser commitment to elections as democratic vehicles is troubling. Experience with elections as instruments of democracy has apparently not been satisfactory. Russians also seem to adhere to a somewhat more participatory vision of democracy, rating assemblies almost as high as elections, and higher than their Canadians counterparts.

When asked specifically about what elections mean to them personally, Russians were less inclined to identify elections as instruments of accountability and policy influence than British respondents[6] and a significant proportion of Russian respondents indicated that elections are vehicles of deception. This scepticism toward elections may have to do more with personal experience than with political vision (or lack thereof). At a minimum one can conclude that Russian respondents are more sceptical about the efficacy of elections and their importance to democracy than are their Canadian and British counterparts, that they may have a more participatory vision of democracy, and that elections as vehicles of democracy are, in practice, viewed with a jaundiced eye.

Table 8: Views of Meaning of Elections in Russia
To what extent do elections mean the following to you personally:

They mean a lot, as a way to...	Russia 1993	Russia 1995	Britain 1987
1. influence policy	27%	45%	60%
2. state an opinion about the situation in the country;	29	43	60
3. choose leaders based on personal qualities;	31	36	
4. deceive the people;	31	34	
5. hold leaders accountable;	23	33	48
6. promote the interests of a social class;	16	33	28
7. keep politicians honest;	22	25	28
8. promote the interests of me and my family;	18	25	34
9. promote the interests of a national or religious group	8	11	

* All-Russia survey, December 1995/January 1996
* Based on the Carleton 1993 and 1995 elections surveys. The 1993 survey was carried out in three regions of Russia; the 1995 survey was an all-Russian representative sample drawn from 19 regions. Data cited from Jon H. Pammett and Joan DeBardeleben, "The Meaning of Elections in Transitional Democracies: Evidence from Russia and Ukraine," *Electoral Studies*, 15.3 (1996): 363-381 and from Jon H. Pammett, "Elections and democracy in Russia," *Communist and Post-Communist Studies*, 32 (1999): 45-60.

Russians also appear to be sceptical of the main national representative body that they elect, the State Duma (the lower house of the national legislature). Surveys carried out by the All-Russian Centre for Public Opinion report that half of Russian respondents in a 2002 survey indicated that the Duma "mainly spends time on unnecessary decisions and squabbling".[7]

Institutional Design and Russian Democracy

What explains the widespread dissatisfaction with democracy in Russia? We have already alluded to some factors, which may be important. These include inflated expectations and the failure of parliamentary elections to influence the composition of the government. But are there more fundamental issues relating to Russian institutional structures that may contribute to an explanation?

A first and very important factor relates to the weakness of political parties in Russia. Only three political parties have won consistent representation in the Duma through the party list portion of the ballot since 1993 (the Communist Party of the Russian Federation, the Yabloko party, and the Liberal Democratic Party or Zhirinovsky Bloc); none of these has ever been in the governing coalition. Neither Russian president has formed his own political party nor made himself accountable to a political party. This position was apparently a matter of principle of Boris Yeltsin, who seemed to desire the appearance of a politician standing above partisan concerns, a stance reflecting the Khruschevian legacy, who defined the Communist Party as representing 'the whole people'. One consequence was the fragmentation of the liberal reform political forces, which continues to this day, since Yeltsin allowed his allies to squabble among themselves about political party formations. Putin, on the other hand, has, to some degree, associated himself with the Unity Party, but he has not defined himself as its leader or representative. This position frees him from accountability to a political party organization and also makes it harder for citizens to see linkages between political parties and the way policy and power is structured.

An additional institutional feature, which may contribute to Russian cynicism about democracy, is the inefficacy of elections as instruments for bringing about changes in government or policy. This has, in part, to due with the structure of Russian political institutions, namely the dual executive. While other countries, most notably France, have a dual executive structure, the Russian case has its own unique features, which may make accountability even more difficult to realize. The President, who is directly elected, appoints the prime minister and the Russian legislature is in a weak position to exercise control over the holder of the post. While the lower house of the Federal Assembly, the Duma, must confirm the appointment, failure to do so eventually can lead to the dissolution of the Duma itself. Thus, the strongest force in the Duma has only a weak capability to exercise positive influence on the government.

Because the prime minister is answerable only in a conditional sense to the Duma and primarily to the President, a model of responsible party government clearly does not apply to the Russian case. Neither the President nor the Duma is an agent of responsible government. On the one hand, while the President is elected on a majoritarian principle, he cannot act effectively and legitimately without gaining the acquiescence of the legislature.[8] On the other hand, the Duma cannot take effective policy leadership, but can rather effectively bloc government initiatives. As was demonstrated in the Yeltsin years, a failure to court opposition in the Duma can lead to immobilism. A certain measure of bargaining or at least cooptation is required for the government or President to gain acceptance of its policies. The government must attend to the Duma, win it over, bargain, and thus achieve adequate support in order to gain acceptance of its legislative program. Most frequently the Duma's influence has taken an obstructive form. President Putin has managed to win more cooperation from the Duma than did President Yeltsin, but it is not clear the degree to which the public can feel represented. Public influence through the Duma is relatively weak precisely because political parties themselves are such weak vehicles of public representation. Furthermore, the rules of the Duma do not assure influence of the opposition on policy and can lead to some fairly divergent outcomes, depending on particular political circumstances. The ability of opposition deputies (particularly Communist deputies) to influence policy-making depends on particular political configurations.

Conclusion

The irony of current Russian political development is that although institutional features make it difficult for elections to serve as very effective vehicles of representation, neither Russian citizens nor politicians seem to question their legitimacy. It could well be argued that elections have had an impact over time by moving the policies of the government away from the radical market reform position toward a more centrist position. These changes were likely made in response to the obstruction to government policies offered by opposition deputies.

Weaknesses in effective representation derive at least in part from the institutional structures, which place the Russian legislature in a weak position to do more than offer a veto point. Other sources of weak representation have to do with the generally weak institutionalization of political parties and their linkages to the public. Exclusion of independent and opposition groups from decision-making can easily occur within the Russian institutional structure. Surprisingly, however, most opposition parties and groups have been co-opted to accept the current institutional structures, suggesting that possibilities for influence have been sufficient to prevent rejection of the rules of the game. Thus, while democracy has not been consolidated and elections are not very effective vehicles of democracy in Russia, they do seem to be 'the only game in town'.

Notes

[1] I am grateful to Inara Gulpe-Laganovska for research assistance for this article.

[2] See Adam Przeworski, *Democracy and the market: political and economic reforms in Eastern Europe and Latin America*, (Cambridge: Cambridge U. Press, 1991).

[3] For discussion of the notion of consolidated democracy, see Bruce Parrott. "Perspectives on postcommunist democratization," in Karen Dawisha and Bruce Parrott, eds, *Democratic Changes and Authoritarian Reactions in Russia, Ukraine, Belarus, and Moldova* (Cambrigde: Cambridge U. Press, 1997) 5-6.

[4] Timothy Colton, *Transitional Citizens: Voters and What Influences Them in Russia*, (Cambridge: Harvard U. Press, 2000); Stephen White, Richard Rose,

and Ian McAllister, *How Russia Votes*, (Chatham: Chatham House Publisher, Inc., 1997).

[5] Richard Rose and Neil Munro, *Elections without Order: Russia's Challenge to Vladimir Putin* (Cambridge: Cambridge U. Press, 2002); Arthur H. Miller, Vicki L. Hesli, and William M. Reisinger, " Conceptions of Democracy Among Mass and Elite in Post-Soviet Societies," *British Journal of Political Science*, 27 (1997): 157-190.

[6] Responses to these types of questions generally do not change quickly, as they reflect underlying value structures rather than responses to current issues.

[7] As reported on the website operated jointly by the Centre for the Study of Public Policy, U. Strathclyde and the Russian Center for Public Opinion and Market Research (VCIOM), <http://www.russiavotes.org/DumaEv.htm> (accessed May 21, 2003).

[8] For an interesting discussion of majoritaG. Bingham Powell. *Elections as Instruments of Democracy: Majoritarian and Proportional Visions* (New Haven; London: Yale U. Press, 2001).

The Russian Presidency and the Process of Democratization

Carlos Canales, Undergraduate Student, York University

After the collapse of the Soviet Union, Russia experienced enormous political, economic, and social instability as decades of communist rule, one party-political system, and a centrally planned economy became part of its past. This country urgently needed new institutions and methods of governance that would guarantee a smooth transition towards democracy and a capitalist economy. Nevertheless, in Russia, there was no previous experience with an institutionalized form of government that would aim for the above.

This quest for a new democratic system began, in fact, before the collapse of the Soviet Union under the auspices of Mikhail Gorbachev. The Soviet ruler championed the creation of a new institution for the Soviet Union that had not existed under communist rule – the Presidency. Mikhail Gorbachev was to become the first and the last President of the Soviet Union. Nonetheless, it is under the works of Boris Yeltsin's leadership that the Russian Presidency was created, consolidated, and strengthened to the extent that it became the most important political institution in post-communist Russia. Paradoxically, while parliamentary institutions as well as structures of civil society continue to be very weak in Russia, a powerful executive institution has emerged, reflecting the country's strong tradition of authoritarian rule.

Not surprisingly, the Russian Presidency has received much attention from scholars, politicians, and political analysts. And, thus, much has been written on this subject from various perspectives. The objective in this particular study is two-fold: a) to examine the Russian presidency in terms of its evolution as well as its institutional design and b) to analyze its contribution to the development of democracy in Russia.

Russia's Political Past and its Legacy

Upon studying today's Russia, it is important to understand where this country is coming from in political terms. Its political history is most definitely an indicator of current and future developements. Russia is a country with a strong heritage of both positive and negative traditions, which penetrate all spheres of political life.

According to many critical Western scholars, "Russia does not have a democratic tradition".[1] And indeed, Russia's "persistent tradition of absolutism in government, the recurrent use of revolutionary violence to solve political problems, and the lack of experience with democratic institutions and constitutional procedures"[2] are some of the attributes that can be invoked. To this executive authoritarian legacy can be added the exclusive position of the 'nomenklatura' and other powerful economic elites as well as the traditional weakness of representative institutions, rule of law, and civil society.

It can also be noted that many key principles of Western-style democracy have traditionally been absent in Russia. In fact, during the

Communist period, notions such as multi-party politics, competitive elections, and accountable government, among others, were either non-existent or not fully developed. Furthermore, before Communism, "there was no pre-communist constitution, as there had been in each of the Baltic republics. There were no pre-communist parties ready to step out of the history books into the centre of public life. And there were no traditions of political organisation and electoral competition, as there had been in most of East Central Europe".[3]

Nevertheless, it must be kept in mind that authoritarian governance is also a phenomenon familiar to Western political experience. In fact, most of the developed Western democracies have gone through authoritarian phases in their history. Russia, can, therefore, overcome its authoritarian past and follow its own path towards democracy as other nations have. Russia has, in fact, already overcome some of these constraints on democracy. As Howard Wiarda points out, "Russia has at present a democratically elected government and many of the classic freedoms",[4] even though it has "a powerful antidemocratic and authoritarian tradition".[5]

Having made some progress towards democracy, Russia can continue to do so following its own path. The challenge is not so much to westernize Russia as to overcome its authoritarian legacy through the development of democratic institutions, which need to be and should be Russian in nature.

Russia's New Presidency: From Gorbachev to Putin

The role of the executive is of utmost importance as a guarantor and promoter of democratic rule within the framework of the rule of law. Its position at the peak of all decisional bodies gives it both the privilege and responsibility to play this role. In Russia, this privilege has been taken for granted and the power of the executive has been overtly abused.

Prior to the current presidential system, the top leadership of the Communist Party of the Soviet Union, CPSU, was the decision-making body in the Soviet Union. At the peak of this party-state apparatus was the Communist Party General or First Secretary, who could also occupy the post of the head of state. Between the CPSU and the population existed the soviets, which "were popularly elected bodies in which, according to Soviet doctrine, legislative and executive power were fused".[6] The CPSU "exercised its power through the soviets and through the executive bodies that were nominally accountable to the soviets".[7]

This system was not abolished all at once; rather, there was a generally gradual transition towards the presidential system of today's Russia. The process in which this was done was, however, not the most democratic or transparent. In fact, "The transformation of Russia's political system after the fall of Communism was determined exclusively by the logic of the political battle being fought at the time, and not by any long-range plans for state-building or by strategic agreements among the main political actors".[8]

Mikhail Gorbachev took the initiative by introducing major changes in the Soviet political system. Handicapped by political instability, economic crisis, and loss of legitimacy, Gorbachev's reforms involved the creation of new legislative and executive branches of government. "Gorbachev created a complicated four-tiered parliament for the USSR, consisting of a huge, 2250-member Congress of People's Deputies, which elected a smaller, full-time parliament called the Supreme Soviet. In turn, the Supreme Soviet was guided by its Presidium, which was overseen by a Chairman".[9] Elections to this new governmental body were held in 1989. In 1990s, elections to similar bodies were held in all 15 republics of the Soviet Union.

Subsequently, Gorbachev also created the office of the President of the Soviet Union. "To overcome the objections of some republican leaders to the establishment of a presidency, Gorbachev agreed to grant them membership in a new body, the Federation Council, which would review policies on inter-ethnic and inter-republican relations".[10] Moreover, "unwilling to risk personal defeat or the strains that a competitive election campaign would place on the nation, Gorbachev insisted that the Congress select the first Soviet president, with subsequent presidential elections to be decided by direct popular vote".[11]

After the Congress of People's Deputies was elected in the Russian Soviet Federative Socialist Republic in 1990, Boris Yeltsin was chosen as its Chairman. Yeltsin and his supporters persuaded the Congress to create a popularly elected Presidency of the Russian Federation, and as a result of the 1991 presidential election, Yeltsin became Russia's first democratically elected head of state. However, it should be noted that "if many Russian deputies supported the introduction of the presidency, it was only because the Congress of the People's Deputies was still legally the supreme organ of power".[12]

After the creation of the Presidency, Yeltsin and his close supporters sought to concentrate as much power as possible in the new institution. "Yet while willing to use power as needed, he also came to rely on the public for support at critical junctures. Thus, while late Soviet period statutes made the Russian president subordinate to the elected legislature, Yeltsin moved forward after the failed August 1991 coup effort to secure extraordinary powers to introduce a radical reform programme".[13] Once again, the means utilized to achieve this goal were quite authoritarian.

The rise of this opportunistic presidency led to a critical confrontation between the executive branch and its legislative counterpart: "A constitutional crisis mounted until the fall of 1993, when Yeltsin issued a decree suspending the parliament, establishing a new legislative body, and calling for new elections in December. [the parliament persisted, and] Yeltsin ultimately called in Russian troops to storm the parliament building. After a brief battle the remaining parliament members surrendered".[14] As Yeltsin had indicated, elections for a new parliament and a referendum on the draft Constitution took place on December 12, 1993.

Given the circumstances, which included the abuse of both political and military power by the presidency, the elections for parliament and the referendum for the new constitution had questionable legitimacy. The population that did go to the polls did so because they needed a parliament and a Constitution to rely on in spite of the political unrest. Moreover, according to election specialists "in all there took part in the elections of December 12, 49 million out of 106.2 registered voters, or 46.1 percent of the total".[15] It was also acknowledged that "last-minute changes to the draft constitution dramatically strengthened presidential power at the expense of parliament".[16]

Thus, Boris Yeltsin created an office that was well above any other governmental or non-governmental body. The presidency has a privileged position due to all the powers that were assigned to it as well as to its superior status vis-à-vis other governmental institutions. This resulted in a very lopsided institutional balance. The predominance of the presidential office adheres to the traditional Russian practice of concentration of power in the hands of the top political executive, be it the Tsar, the Communist Party's General Secretary, or the President. As

Archie Brown points out, "the presidency was a completely new institution in Russia's political tradition, but still, by a circuitous route, through the twisted paths of the political struggle, it led back to the autocratic tradition".[17] Brown also states that the creation of the presidency "was a movement in a direction typical for Russia, towards a system where power is personified completely and embodied in one person".[18]

In the evolution of events, the ultimate outcome was a winner-takes-all scenario. Thus, "the president predominates constitutionally over parliament not because of some coherent idea of the proper role of the chief executive, but because it was the Supreme Soviet (the State Duma's predecessor) and not the presidency that lost the great institutional power struggle of 1993".[19] This was a battle that could not be constitutionally, politically or even morally justified: "Above all, it imposed a strongly presidential system for which there was no national consensus, and which raised political and constitutional difficulties of its own".[20]

Moreover, "Yeltsin and his supporters shaped the post-Soviet system and created an all-powerful presidency, with Yeltsin's own constitutionally legitimated transfer of power to Vladimir Putin at the end of the 1999 setting yet another precedent in the consolidation of the new system".[21] Once Putin took power, he made no effort whatsoever to reverse any of the authoritarian developments that had taken place prior to his tenure of office, au contraire, he envisioned concentrating even more power in his office. "Shortly after assuming the presidency on 7 May 2000, he delivered a television address to the nation that called for a dictatorship of law to restore strong and centralized government".[22] With concrete actions, the new president "introduced bills that promised to return Russia to a more traditional Moscow-centred and one-man-centred style of rule".[23]

Although the specific political events differ from one ruler to the next, in essence the actions taken are quiet similar. They include autocratic-type rule, abuse of power leading to excessive use of force in some instances, and using citizens not as active participants in policy-making, but as the mass base for realization of projects ordered from above. It is, thus, of crucial importance for the future of Russian democracy to reform the political system so as to control and counteract this authoritarian tendency.

The Institutional Design of the Russian Presidency

The new Russian constitution, like many constitutions of modern democratic states, "specifies a separation of state power into three branches, ensures 'ideological pluralism' by proscribing any state-sponsored ideology, and maintains a separation of church and state".[24] These are basic principles that are shared by democracies around the globe in their attempt to avoid the possibility of the rise of authoritarian regimes.

Nonetheless, in Russia the actual division of powers among the branches of government is unequal. The executive has overwhelming powers over the legislature and the judiciary. It is imperative to emphasize at this point that this is a political design that can function well elsewhere, but not necessarily in Russia.

As Stephen White argues, "the formal powers of the Russian president are extremely far-reaching. He makes appointments to almost all positions of importance, including the powerful Security Council and government itself (he appoints the prime minister 'with the agreement of the State Duma', and on his proposal appoints and dismisses other ministers)".[25] In practice, "as the experience of Yeltsin regime aptly demonstrated, the president has the power to appoint and dismiss the prime minister, deputy prime ministers and other ministers, as well as dismiss the government overall".[26] What entitles the president to such extensive power is the fact that "unlike the French system of possible "cohabitation", where a prime minister heading the government has a power base at least partially independent of the president, the Russian prime minister must maintain the president's confidence to remain in office".[27]

Moreover, "the president has the power to dissolve the Duma and call new elections".[28] He/she also has "the right to issue decrees that have the force of law".[29] And, "indeed, many controversial political decisions, such as the September 1993 dissolution of parliament and the

December 1994 intervention in Chechnya, were taken by decree".[30] These presidential decrees are not only used to impose political actions of great magnitude and controversy but are also excessively utilized, as it was demonstrated with over 1,500 decrees issued during the Yeltsin's regime alone.

The president's role is not limited to the executive function; he/she is also at the core of the legislative process. The president can, in fact, initiate and reject legislation. Should the president reject a bill, a two-thirds majority vote from both houses is needed to override the presidential veto – a majority difficult or impossible to achieve, given the degree of control the President has over the legislature.

Moreover, the President also has the power to appoint members of the Constitutional Court. Further, "the Constitution permits the President to use 'reconciliatory procedures' to settle differences between the federal and regional authorities.[31] President Putin used this power actively to recentralize Russian state authority. "In several particularly egregious cases of a conflict of laws, Putin acted immediately to annul regional legislation or send warning letters to governors".[32]

As for institutional means to control the presidency, they are almost non-existent. John P. Willerton Jr clearly and appropriately indicated in his work on the Russian presidency, "what makes the presidency hegemonic is not only the fact that its position is legally superior to that of other bodies, but the institutional independence and freedom of manoeuvre the president possesses".[33] It is true that "the president must be elected; but he is not accountable to the Federal Assembly, and can only be removed from office for 'high treason or other grave state crime' after a very complicated process has been invoked"[34], which involves both houses of parliament as well as the Constitutional Court. Moreover, "If the Duma passes a vote of no confidence in the government, the president may either dissolve the Duma or dismiss the government".[35]

Thus, the Russian presidency has enormous power subject to very few limitations. One might argue that the features of the Russian presidency are similar to those of Western presidential systems, for instance, the American system – and that if this design functions well in other democracies, it should also be viable for Russia. But this argument reflects the questionable westernization assumption that what is good for the West is good elsewhere. This institutional design is not placed within a vacuum but within a very specific historical and cultural context. In so far as democratic development in Russia continues to be hampered by strong authoritarian traditions, the current institutional design does not impede such tendency but rather facilitate it. Thus, the president's extraordinary role in Russian politics presents a very serious challenge to the development of Russian democracy.

The Russian Presidency and the Process of Democratization: Are They Compatible?

The Russian presidency has, as John P. Willerton Jr. indicates, "evolved into a powerful institution affecting all aspects of Russian political life".[36] Unfortunately, the evolution of the Russian presidency did not result from any strategic plan for democratic development. As discussed by a critical scholar of post-communist Russia, "rather than study the complex and subtle ways in which democratic institutions shape incentives and sustain themselves over the long haul, Russian leaders have preferred to indulge in superficial manipulations aimed at securing immediate advantages for themselves and their factions".[37] This was most definitely the case of Boris Yeltsin and, to a certain extent, Vladimir Putin, who accepted the existing setup and strengthened the Presidency even more.

But what is democracy precisely? One of the best known definitions is given by Robert Dahl, who emphasizes three aspects: "1) organized contestation through regular, free, and fair elections; 2) the right of virtually all adults to vote and contest for office; and 3) freedom of press, assembly, speech, petition, and organization".[38] Although, all these elements of democracy have been questionably fulfilled in Russia, this country cannot be perceived as a complete democracy. Neil Munro and Richard Rose offer an interesting approach to identifying democracies, which complements Dahl's definition. Their approach is also appropriate for states such as Russia, which are currently going through the process of democratic development. According to Munro and

Rose, "a completely democratic state must meet two conditions: it must be a modern, rule-of-law state and the government must be chosen by free elections. If only one of these conditions is met, then a regime is incompletely democratic".[39]

Under such definition, Russia is not yet a completely democratic state. Munro and Rose note that "leaders of new regimes are often more concerned with building their own power than with institutionalizing a rule-of-law state that imposes constraints on the power they claim by virtue of election".[40] Rule of law enables a strong presidency while constraining possibilities of its abuse. If there are no constraints, the chief political executive is free to rule with absolute power. "In framing a government, which is to be administered by men over men, the great difficulty lies in this: you must first enable the government to control the governed; and in the next place oblige it to control itself".[41]

Russia is at a crucial moment in its process of building a democratic state since the relatively undemocratic constitutional system recently created by Boris Yeltsin is still in place. President Putin had the option of proposing constitutional reforms, which would limit presidential powers and thereby further the process of building both the rule of law and democracy. Instead, he continued to follow the path dictated by Boris Yeltsin. Moreover, "should Putin succeed in the campaign to strengthen the presidency and the central state, there is a risk that an attempt to rationalize state authority may degenerate into a new authoritarianism. One cannot rule out the rise of a future leader- a statist with a world-view uncluttered by liberal values-who is willing to use the heightened powers of the Russian presidency to silent all opposition."[42] This goes back to the authoritarian Russian tradition "of accountability to the tsar rather than by the tsar".[43]

How can Russia overcome this authoritarian legacy at the executive level? Most definitely, the answer is not to import a democratic tradition from elsewhere. The solution to this problem must be found at home. Unfortunately, "post-soviet Russian society continues to wrestle with this historical past of executive domination and public submission, yet in the midst of ongoing turbulent transformational politics, many Russians continue to desire – as consistently revealed in opinion surveys – a strong, stabilising hand at the state's helm".[44]

This situation needs to be dealt with at all levels of state and society. Both the government and the governed must come to the realization that what is needed is not a strong (authoritarian) leader but one that is willing to govern with all the limitations that the virtue of elections provides. Thus, what is needed is a leader that submits him/herself to real rule of law. In order to achieve this, the institutional design of the government needs to be reworked, especially in terms of limiting the power of the presidency and its dominance over the other government institutions. Such constraints should be based on the limitation of executive powers and institutional accountability.

These changes might seem unattainable in Russia, especially because this revolution must come from above, as the executive must give up power. However, we can cite the precedent set by Mikhail Gorbachev, who initiated liberal reforms which were considered unthinkable at the time. The civil society, interest groups, and the representative bodies of the state must all work together to make the President acknowledge that changes need to be made. In spite of their prolonged weakness, it is imperative to start "by slowly nurturing home-grown, local, and indigenous institutions, which are often the only viable ones in the society, and carefully cultivating them meanwhile encouraging economic, social, and political growth - until they have a chance to flower into full-fledged democracy".[45] After all, home-grown democracy has a better chance to prosper and last than imposed or imitated democracy.[46]

Notes
[1] Howard Wiarda, *Comparative Democracy and Democratization,* (Harcourt College Publishers, 2002) 62.
[2] Gregory Mahler, *Comparative Politics: An Institutional and Cross-National Approach,*(Prentice Hall, 2000) 344.
[3] Stephan White, *Developments in Russian Politics,* (Duke U. Press, Durham, 2001) 1.
[4] Wiarda, 12.
[5] Ibid.
[6] White, 42.
[7] Ibid.
[8] Archie Brown, *Contemporary Russian Politics,* (Oxford U. Press, Oxford, 2001) 14.
[9] White, 42.
[10] Brown, 33.
[11] Ibid.
[12] Ibid,15.

[13] White, 25.

[14] Ibid, 69.

[15] Brown, 59.

[16] Ibid, 37.

[17] Brown, 14.

[18] Ibid.

[19] Ibid, 19.

[20] White, 12.

[21] Ibid, 22.

[22] Brown, 87.

[23] Ibid, 82.

[24] Wiarda, 69.

[25] White, 13.

[26] Ibid, 28.

[27] Ibid, 32.

[28] Wiarda, 69.

[29] White, 13.

[30] Ibid, 29.

[31] Wiarda, 70.

[32] Brown, 89.

[33] White, 27.

[34] Ibid, 13.

[35] Wiarda, 70.

[36] White, 21.

[37] Brown, 19.

[38] Wiarda, 7.

[39] Neil Munro et al, *Elections without Order,* (Cambridge U. Press, Cambridge, 2002) 42.

[40] Ibid, 43.

[41] Ibid, 44.

[42] Brown, 96.

[43] Munro et al, 46.

[44] White, 22.

[45] Wiarda, 9.

[45] For other sources used in this essay that were not cited, please see as follows: Mark Kesselman, Joel Krier and C.S. Allen, *European Politics in Transition,* (Houghton Mifflin, New York, 2002); Peter Reddaway and Dmitri Glinski, *The Tragedy of Russia's Reforms: Market Bolshevism Against Democracy,* (The United State Institute of Peace, Washington, DC, 2001); The Constitution of the Russian Federation

<http://www.departments.bucknell.edu/russian/const/constit.html>; Further research, interviews, and lectures received at the Institute of the U.S. and Canadian Studies, Russian Academy of Sciences, Moscow, Russia <http://iskran.iip.net/engl/index-en.html>; and the Embassy of the Russian Federation in <Canadahttp://www.rusembcanada.mid.ru/>

Reforming Russia's Judiciary

Professor Peter H. Solomon, Jr., University of Toronto

As of the start of 2003, the process of judicial reform in the Russian Federation was in high gear. This was due in large part to the priority given by President Putin to the strengthening of courts and law, as reflected in: the Federal Program for the Development of the Courts, political support for the adoption of new procedure codes, and the efforts to establish legal hierarchy (through the harmonization of laws and the distribution of governmental functions through law). Today, I present some of the highlights of the current court reform project, placing it in the context of the past decade; and then argue that the ultimate success of these efforts at institutional change depends upon the degree to which they are accompanied, sooner or later, by cultural changes and changes in the nature of governance.

The Yeltsin Legacy

In the Yeltsin years, much was done to reduce the dependency of judges upon outside forces, such as local and regional bosses, and to empower the courts. Judges on most courts received life appointments and became subject to removal only for cause by Judicial Qualification Collegia composed only of their peers. The financing of the courts became an exclusively federal responsibility, and new judicial departments subordinate to the judiciary took over court administration from the Ministry of Justice. At the same time, courts assumed a great deal of new and important jurisdiction, ranging from constitutional and commercial matters to the crucial domain of administrative justice. Citizens gained the right to complain about the legality of acts of officials and even normative acts themselves. By the end of the decade, they were bringing a huge number of suits against the government (in regular, arbitrazh and military courts), and for the most part successfully.

Nonetheless, there remained obstacles to the achievement of independent and powerful courts. From 1997 regional governments again had a voice in judicial selection, and could veto the promotion of judges to higher courts or the appointment of chairs of courts. The failure of the federal government to deliver all of the funds assigned to the courts led court chairs in 1997 and 1998 to seek and obtain supplementary funding from local and regional governments and even from private sponsors – thereby raising the specter of renewed dependencies. The authority of courts, especially in the constitutional and commercial realms, was hurt by difficulties in assuring implementation of their decisions. As if this were not enough, a significant part of the public did not trust the courts, viewing them as inefficient if not also corrupt.

Putin and the Courts

Vladimir Putin was determined to change this situation and achieve courts in Russia that would be respected and trusted, as well as provide a reliable framework for investors. During the winter of 2001, a high level commission under deputy head of the presidential administration Dmitrii Kozak wrestled with this challenge and produced a set of recommendations most of which were realized in legislation at the end of the year. To strengthen the accountability of judges (and the appearance that corruption and inefficiency were being addressed), jurists from outside the judiciary were added to the Qualification Collegia, the rules for removing judicial immunity from prosecution simplified, and chairs of courts limited to fixed terms in office. To strengthen the independence of judges, regional governments were removed from the appointment and promotion process. But the most significant change was the adoption of the Federal Program for the Development of the Courts for 2002 to 2006 that dramatically increased federal funding of the courts. The program has raised the salaries of judges significantly and phased out most of their perks and benefits, some of which were given at the discretion of the court chair. The program has also provided funds for hiring new judges (especially justices of the peace) and clerks (pomoshchniki suda), for the education of judges, and for repairing and modernizing court buildings and computerizing the court system; and paid for the extension of jury trials to regional and republican level courts through the Russian Federation. The extraordinary new federal funding is meant not only to improve court operations but also to reduce financial dependency on regional and local governments.

Among the reform initiatives currently underway are two of special importance and interest – the justice of the peace courts and the new Criminal Procedure Code. Although, conceived as a revival from the Tsarist past that would bring justice closer to the people, the establishment of JP courts from late 1999 fulfilled the desire of top judges to expand the judicial system and relieve caseload pressure; and, as of the end of 2002, some 5,000 justices (each serving a geographical district) had begun handling a high volume of cases of low complexity. Justices of the peace in Russia are regular, full time professional judges whose salaries are paid by the federal government, but whose courts belong to the subjects of the Federation, which are responsible for financing their administration and selecting their justices. The JPs jurisdiction includes most divorce and family cases, disputes over wages and failures to repair apartments, violations of tax law, all suits of moderate value, and the bulk of criminal offences bringing punishments of no more than three years confinement, as well as all administrative infractions. As a result the JPs are hearing on average 70% of civil cases and 30% of criminal cases, thereby relieving the district courts of a lot of caseload, and giving their judges time to consider complicated cases more carefully. Admittedly, district courts take cases on appeal from the JPs, but only three percent of their decisions are challenged. In many places, the JPs are becoming strained, and at the start of 2003 plans were underway to expand the system to 9,500 justices, or one third of the whole judicial corps in the Russian Federation. Already, JPs have become the court with which most citizens have contact. But their quality varies dramatically, depending upon the degree of support provided by the various subject governments.

After more than a decade of struggle, a new Criminal Procedure Code went into operation in July 2002, some of whose provisions were revolutionary, and whose implementation is still being opposed by the police. The expansion of trial by jury (which routinely produces acquittals rates in the double digits as opposed to a fraction of one percent) is well known. But there are more important novelties. One is the fulfilment of the constitutional requirement of exclusively judicial approval of pre-trial detention. In practice, this has led to a sharp and apparently lasting drop in the number and percentage of accused persons placed in custody, partly because of judge refusals (15% of the time) but even more because procurators are unwilling to request detention where the grounds are shaky. Given the horrible state of the investigatory prisons (SIZO), this is a big achievement. As part of its emphasis on adversarial procedure, the new Code also requires that procurators argue every case in court and approve all indictments, and the Code eliminated a favourite ending of cases that came apart, the infamous return to supplementary investigation. As a result, procurators have started to screen cases coming from the police, and now throw out weak or poorly prepared cases, so that the overall number of criminal cases has decreased. Even so, the rate of acquittal has doubled since last summer (now averaging close to 2%), and many more cases are stopped by judges. The fairness of criminal justice in Russia is increasing, for weak cases presented by police (often incompetently prepared or launched under pressure) are no longer as likely to result in convictions. Another novelty in the new UPK is a shortened trial following confession. To be sure, Soviet style plea bargaining is limited to charges bringing up to five years, but it is working well in practice and producing sentences of greater leniency than required by the law. To ensure that the UPK is properly implemented and adjusted where appropriate, a major monitoring is taking place under the guidance of Duma deputy Elena Miziulina.

I have touched on only a small number of current judicial reform initiatives. Efforts also are underway to strengthen the 'arbitrazh' courts that handle commercial disputes, including the taxation of firms, to implement a new civil procedure code, and to establish new brand administrative courts. And there are a number of projects funded by Western governments (including especially Canada) and by the World Bank aimed at modernizing the functioning of courts and inter alia removing from judges and chairs of courts non-judicial functions that interfere with the impartiality of adjudication.

Meta-institutional (Cultural) Challenges

To succeed in achieving courts that are fair, efficient, trusted and respected, judicial reform needs to produce cultural change and to benefit from cultural changes within public life; more generally.

To start, there is the challenge of changing the mentalities of judges, to ensure that they (and especially younger judges) internalize the concept of judicial independence, judicial ethics, and above all a commitment to applying legal principles and rights that exist beyond the letter of particular laws. Judges need to reach beyond the strict positivism of the civil law tradition and absorb the newer European recognition that law (pravo) consists of more than the laws of the state (zakony) and gives pride of place to rights of a transcendental kind, which have been built into European wide legal documents that the Russian Federation has endorsed. Despite the ambitions of the new Academy of Justice, so far newly appointed judges receive only a one month training course; this does not promote the values I refer to.

Even more serious is the lag of public appreciation of the courts behind the real advances in their performance. In the new millennium polls record public attitudes toward courts in Russia as ambivalent and sceptical, if not downright negative. How a public perceives its courts reflects concern with the fairness of the courts' decisions; with accessibility to the courts; and with the efficiency of court operations. Obviously, if the public believes judges to be corrupt or serving the rich, it will not hold courts in high esteem. Accessibility also matters. A 2001 survey by VTsIOM found that 80% of well off persons in Russia believed that courts would defend their rights, but that less than 20% of persons with low education and incomes shared this belief. At the same time, poll data from Western countries indicates that the perceived efficiency of courts correlates closely with their standing in the mind of the public. In countries like Denmark, Finland and Austria, around half of the public sees courts as efficient and even more trust their courts. In

Belgium, where only 17% see their courts as efficient, only 22% trust them.

How can Russia, a country where the social legitimacy of courts was never high, become less like Belgium and more like Finland? On the one hand, it is vital to improve the actual fairness, accessibility, and efficiency of the courts. On the other hand, it is important to better inform the public about how the courts are improving. Too often the Russian public is ignorant about what the courts can do. A poll conducted in 1997 revealed that only 20% of Russians thought that they were likely to succeed if they complained in court against a government official, whereas the actual rate of satisfaction stood around 80%! As I argued in Moscow last week at a roundtable meeting of Russian judges and court administrators with Western donors, public education about the courts represents a key response. Press officers need to be established not only in judicial departments but also in large courts; and courts of all kinds should place more of their decisions on websites (now done only on an experimental basis). In short, improving public esteem for courts in the Russian Federation requires a new level of transparency about their operations – however foreign this may be to Russian and even European traditions.

Finally, the achievement of fair and trusted courts cannot happen independently of changes in other parts of government that connect with law. One is overcoming the traditional weakness in Russia of legal prerogatives. Too often roles and agencies have functions rather than legally defined powers, and relationships among actors and governments are defined through personal connections rather than rules. President Putin's current effort to use law to specify the concrete responsibilities of different levels of government in the RF represents an admirable if partial response. Another law-related challenge is the need to transform the work of government officials in Russia so that they become a public service based upon the application of rules (a Weberian bureaucracy) rather than an amalgam of fiefdoms based upon clientelism serving for the most part sectoral and private interests. Perhaps, through compartmentalization it is possible to have in Russia fair and respected courts coexisting with public administration that is, or is perceived to be, corrupt. But I would not count on it.

Conclusion

In their classic treatise on democratic transitions Juan Linz and Al Stepan argue that consolidated democracy requires rule of law, but offer no hints as to how that blessed and ill defined state of affairs might emerge in a country where law had served as a mere instrument of rule and courts were dependent on political authority. A satisfactory theory of legal transition has yet to be developed, although elements of one are in the air. That there must be demand for law among key elites, and not only a supply of good laws and legal institutions, is accepted by many. And, as I have suggested, legal and judicial reform will not reach fulfilment should they take place in a vacuum. Changes in public attitudes and changes in the practices of government itself must sooner or later come to reinforce and support changes in the institutions of the law.

All this suggests that the battle for the courts will be one of decades rather than years. Just as the successes of the Judicial Reform of 1864 were recognized and celebrated only in 1914, after fifty years, so the real meaning and impact of the efforts of reformers under Yeltsin and Putin will be clear only well into the future.[1]

Notes
[1] To read more about the subjects presented in this essay and for citations to relevant materials, see: Peter H. Solomon, Jr.: "Putin's Judicial Reform: Making Judges Accountable as well as Independent", *East European Constitutional Review*, ii:2 (Winter/spring 2002), 117-124; "Judicial Power in Russia: Through the Prism of Administragive Justice", unpublished paper (August 2002); "The New Justice of the Peace Courts in the Russian Federation: A Cornerstone of Judicial Reform?," *Demokratizatsiya*, 11.3 (Summer, 2003); "Advancing and Enriching Judicial Reform in the Russian Federation: An Outisder Perspective", unpublished paper (February 2003); and Peter H. Solomon, Jr. and Todd S. Foglesong, *Courts and Transition in Russia: The Challenge of Judicial Reform*, (Boulder, Colorado: Westview, 2002).

Engendering Democracy in Russia
Professor Valerie Sperling, Clark University

Building democracy in Russia is a gendered process. This paper briefly treats three aspects of Russia's ongoing struggle with democratization, showing that each of these aspects is gendered, and asking where women are in each of these processes. First, I discuss political representation, exploring women's participation in the decision-making bodies of the country. Then, I examine women's representation 'outside' of high politics, looking at civil society and women's organizations in particular, and at the challenges they face in trying to gain financial support and a popular 'constituency' – a concept crucial to democracy. Finally, I describe a Russian women's organization called the Committee of Soldiers' Mothers, which is struggling to bring about one of the central aspects of democratization, namely, implementing the rule of law.

Political Representation

Women's representation in the political bodies of the Russian state – in the parliament, the executive branch, and in local government – is limited. One concept that can be useful here is the 'gender gap' – a shorthand way of describing the under-representation of women in political positions. I should say from the start that the proportion of men and women as elected and appointed politicians in nearly all countries is highly skewed, with men dominating the political field across the board.

This is true of Russia as well. The gender gap is so dramatic that Russia's political elite has been described as a 'male club'. As one illustration of that exclusivity, between 1996-1999, there was only one woman in the upper house of Russia's parliament.[1]

The story of women's representation in the lower house of Russia's parliament over the last ten years is not entirely linear. Back in October 1993, after Yeltsin had the military shell the Russian parliament, it was announced that there would be elections in just a few months to a new legislative body, the Duma. At that time, one of the women's organizations in Russia wrote to all of the parties that were planning to field candidates, to inquire as to what their party platforms were going to say about women's concerns; these concerns included disproportionately female unemployment, the low representation of women in politics, and widespread violence against women, among others. Only a few political parties bothered to respond, and the most memorable response came from Zhirinovsky, who said his party's position on women's problems was that, if his party won the elections, it would provide a man for each woman; it would make sure that no woman would be left without a man. This was a way of dismissing women's concerns, claiming that women's problems could be reduced to the presence or lack of a 'muzhik', of a man, in their lives. This women's organization found Zhirinovsky's response and others to be rather unsatisfying and decided to form their own electoral bloc for the 1993 elections, called Women of Russia. In a surprising development, Women of Russia attained roughly 8% of the vote, and their bloc crossed the threshold into the Duma. That success brought the percentage of women in the Duma to just over 11 percent [2]. However, the percentage of women in Russia's Duma has declined since then, and today is only about 7 percent, so there is a gender gap in women's representation at the national level.

There is also a gender gap at the regional level in Russia, where parliamentary bodies are dominated by men. As of June 1997, legislatures in several of Russia's regions contained no women at all. In four of Russia's 89 regions women's representation reached 30%, but, overall, across Russia's subnational legislatures, only 9 percent of the deputies were female as of February 1999.[2] Relatively few women are being elected to Russia's law-making bodies.

Within the executive branch, the gender gap is even more dramatic. In 1999, there was only one woman among Russia's governors and heads of republic governments and administrations (the governor of the Koriak autonomous okrug). Within the state bureaucracy, the 'glass ceiling' largely keeps women at lower levels of power. And as of 1999, women occupied just over one percent of the leadership positions in Russia's executive bodies, working as ministers or heading state committees.[3]

Women are clearly disadvantaged within Russia's state administration, and that disadvantage may increase under Putin. One

Russian sociologist, Olga Kryshtanovskaia, has argued that approximately one third of new appointees at the deputy minister level under Putin's administration over the last three years were formerly employed in the military or intelligence fields.[4] Those fields are highly male dominated. If Russia's military and security/intelligence institutions are becoming an increasingly significant route to political power, then women's path into decision-making positions may be necessarily limited.

Civil Society and Women's Organizations

Citizens, however, have alternative ways of getting their voices heard in politics. And although women are often excluded from high-level politics, they tend to play a large role in the nongovernmental (NGO) sector, which is less prestigious and lower paid than the business sector or high politics. But the NGO sector is nonetheless crucial for the development and entrenchment of civil society. And civil society is an essential element of any stable, consolidated democracy; it can serve to put a check on state power by encouraging citizen responsibility and activism, and thereby promoting civic engagement. American sociologist Myra Marx Ferree refers to the work of civil society as the 'housework' of politics, the unrecognized, largely unrewarded backbone of a democracy that keeps the politicians in check, keeps them responsible to the people, and thereby keeps democracy working.[5]

What have women been doing in this realm of civic activism in Russia? Since the start of Gorbachev's glasnost policy in the late 1980s, women's groups have been organizing. In 1991, approximately 200 women joined together for the first independent women's conference in Russia, the Independent Women's Forum. The organizers chose the term "independent" to reflect the fact that the conference was not organized by the communist party; it was organized from below, through women's networking. Organizing this conference was a fairly risky venture – after all, at the time, in 1991, grassroots organizing had been illegal until quite recently, and the state was still troubled by the idea of women – or anyone else – organizing on their own. On the eve of the conference, a popular newspaper published an article saying that the conference was going to be a meeting of 'overexcited lesbians', and parents in the town where the conference was to be held were warned to keep their children off the streets.[6] Now, just over a decade later, there are hundreds of women's organizations operating in Russia, ranging from small women's studies research centers in Moscow and St. Petersburg and other major cities, to political advocacy groups that lobby on women's issues, to organizations of women journalists and other professionals; to women's employment training organizations, businesswomen's clubs, charities, and single mothers' groups – and there are a growing number of rape crisis centers and domestic violence hotlines in Russia's major cities.

The slogan of the First Independent Women's Forum was 'Democracy minus women is not democracy', suggesting that one central aspect of women's organizing in Russia has been to provide a voice for women in the public sphere, to raise problems that male politicians seem content to ignore. Such problems include the dramatic collapse in women's social, economic, and political status in Russia since the early 1990s.

There is no lack of issues for women's movement groups in Russia to pursue. But the women's movement is beset by many challenges, including a lack of organizing experience, a lack of financial support, and one challenge that confronts every social movement, namely, how to frame the issues so that they will draw the attention of the public, and resonate with the public in order to get widespread support.

The challenge of fundraising is a particularly interesting one for the women's movement in Russia.[7] In the mid-1990s, in the course of carrying out research for my book on the women's movement, every women's group I interviewed complained about a lack of money. For these organizations, even the cost of a fax machine was too high, and only a very few could afford an office. One of the reasons for this is that the women's groups are not involved in fundraising within Russia because the fundraising tactics that most organizations use in the West are not likely to be effective or even plausible for Russia. Whereas NGOs in the West want to raise money, they generally reach out to their members, or to a list of people that they believe might be inclined to donate some money to them – and they request such donations through a direct mail campaign. Those who receive the mailing and choose to donate are likely to write a check, and put it in the mail, or to give the NGO permission to take a certain amount of money through a credit card. This process of 'checkbook activism', long familiar in the West, is not yet established in Russia, and the costs of a direct mail campaign would be beyond the realm of possibility for Russian women's groups.

As a partial result of this economic-structural issue, many women's groups are funded by grants from foreign foundations, such as the Open Society Institute (Soros) and the Ford Foundation, and from foreign governmental funds (such as US government funds, distributed through USAID, and Canadian government funding). This funding is critical for Russian women's organizations; civil society, in order to function as a check on the state, needs money in order to organize. Yet there are unexpected side effects of this funding process.

One side effect is a certain amount of competition between women's groups for foreign grants, since many groups find themselves applying for the same, limited pot of money. Another relevant side-effect of foreign funding is that many of the Russian women's movement activists have learned to use an English-language vocabulary to describe their work, in part because that work may benefit from the support of foreign feminists as well as foreign funders. Given the absence of domestic support for their organizations, this is an adaptive choice. Women's movement activists, especially in Moscow and St. Petersburg, refer to 'gender issues', having adopted the word 'gender' from English directly into Russian – as 'gender' – because there is no equivalent term in Russian. One of the problems for constituency-building, then is that some of the vocabulary of the women's movement will be inaccessible to the average Russian citizen.

Thus, there are incentives for women activists in Russia to speak to their English-speaking audiences abroad, rather than to their potential mass audience at home. This can become a vicious circle for a social movement. If the focus remains on doing outreach to foreigners for funding, then domestic support from women at home may never be built. This has ramifications for democracy and the building of a constituency.

The women's movement in Russia is sometimes dismissed as being a non-Russian phenomenon, a movement imported from the West, a movement that does not belong. This happens not only in Russia – feminism or any ideology that promises to change the existing balance of power is almost always blamed on outside agitators, in countries across the globe. However, the fact that women's groups are targeted in this way as being 'foreign' is reinforced by the fact that many women's organizations in Russia are largely detached from a domestic constituency. These organizations are not mobilisational – they are not mass organizations, and they tend to lack dues-paying members, for the above-described reasons.

This phenomenon of a lack of domestic constituency for the women's movement in Russia echoes a similar problem among Russia's political parties. They tend to be weak when it comes to defining their programs, and they tend to be disconnected from constituencies. This only exacerbates the detachment of the population from politics, and bodes poorly for the democratization process in Russia on the whole.

Democratization and The Committee of Soldiers' Mothers

The Committee of Soldiers' Mothers is one women's organization active in Russia at present, which enjoys a grassroots base.[8] But the Committee's goal does not concern improving women's status; rather, it is focused on repairing several gaps in Russia's democracy. The Committee got its start in the late 1980s, protesting against the Soviet Union's war in Afghanistan, and against the brutal hazing process within the military. At this point, their main activities still include tracking deaths and injuries from hazing; they also counsel draft-age men and their parents about their rights, and they lobby for alternative service for those who do not want to serve in the Russian military. With regard to the current war going on in Chechnya, the Committee of Soldiers' Mothers tries to spread accurate information about the war, by holding demonstrations, and press conferences. They further argue that the war in Chechnya is violating human rights, especially against civilians.[9]

The Committee of Soldiers' Mothers argues that such acts are incompatible with democracy. Instead, they call upon the state to obey the rule of law, to be transparent and honest with the population, to uphold human rights, and freedom of information. And in their actions the Soldiers' Mothers model this behaviour. When they lobby draft boards on behalf of their clientele, they argue strictly on the basis of Russian laws. Representatives of the Russian military and state have predictably responded to the Committee of Soldiers' Mothers by labelling them as CIA agents.[10]

This presents another instance of portraying a women's organization as 'foreign', as being alien to Russia, because they are challenging the state and the existing power hierarchy.

In sum, I would argue that it is precisely this kind of challenge to the state that is a crucial aspect of building democracy. The more women organize on critical issues, the more citizens will become accustomed to the idea that the state, ultimately, should be accountable to them. This is a concept that was obviously anathema to the Soviet state, and one that is all too distant even from established democracies. Without a strong judicial system to hold executive power in check, and in the absence of a media that is able to safely portray the seamy underside of executive actions, it is inevitably up to the people to hold their elected leaders accountable, and to overcome whatever hesitations they may have about being actively engaged in the public sphere. This is one of the challenges central to the democratization process in Russia.

Notes

[1] Nadezhda Shvedova, "Why has there been no real progress toward improving women's status in all spheres of life?" *We/My*, 14.30, (2001).

[2] Ibid.

[3] Ibid.

[4] "Women, intellectuals lose under Putin," Radio Free Europe/Radio Library, September 19, 2002.

[5] Nadezhda Shvedova, "Why has there been no real progress toward improving women's status in all spheres of life?" *We/My*, 14.30, (2001).

[6] Valerie Sperling, Myra Marx Ferree, Barbara Risman, "Constructing Global Feminism: Transnational Advocacy Networks and Russian Women's Activism", *Signs* 26.4, (2001): 1156-1186.

[7] Valaire Sperling, Organizing Women in Contemporary Russia: Endengering Transition (Cambridge U. Press, 1999).

[8] Ibid, 220-256.

[9] Valerie Sperling, "The Last Refuge of a Scoundrel: Patriotism, Militarism, and the Russian National Idea", *Nations and Nationalism* 9.2, (2003): 235-253.

[10] On the violation of human rights in Chechnya, see Anna Politkovskaya, *A Dirty War* (London: Harvill Press, 1999).

Circumstances Versus Policy Choices: Why Has Economic Performance of FSU States Been so Poor?

Professor Vladimir Popov, Carleton University

After the Soviet Union collapsed (December 1991) and market reforms were initiated, the economic performance of the successor states was more than disappointing. By the end of the 1990s output (GDP) had fallen by about 50% as compared to the highest pre-recession level of 1989 (fig. 1), investment dropped even more, income inequalities rose greatly so that real incomes declined dramatically for the majority of the population, death rates increased by about 50%, whereas life expectancy declined markedly. In Russia output fell by 45% in 1989-98, death rates increased from 1% in the 1980s to 1.5% in 1994 and stayed at this high level thereafter, which was equivalent to over 700,000 additional deaths annually. Over the period of several years such population losses could be likened to the impact of the big war.

During the Second World War, national income in the USSR fell only by 20% in 1940-42, recovered to its 1940 level in 1944, fell again by 20% in 1944-46 (during the conversion of the defense industry) but exceeded its 1940 level nearly by 20% already in 1948. In some of the FSU states that were affected by military conflicts (Armenia, Azerbaijan, Georgia, Moldova, Russia and Tajikistan) GDP in 2000 was only 30 to 50% of its pre-transition levels; in Ukraine even without the military conflict GDP fell by nearly two thirds (fig. 1). In another comparison, in

East European countries (EE) the reduction of output continued for 2-4 years and totaled 20 to 30%, whereas in China and Vietnam there was no transformational recession at all – on the contrary, from the very outset of reforms economic growth accelerated.

'Post factum', the reduction of output that occurred in the FSU during the 1990s should be considered as the exceptional case in world economic history. Never and nowhere, to the best of my knowledge, has there occurred such a dramatic decline in output, living standards and life expectancy without extraordinary circumstances, such as wars, epidemics, or natural disasters. Even during the Great Depression (1929-33) GDP in Western countries on average fell by some 30% and by the end of the 1930s recovered to its pre-recession levels.

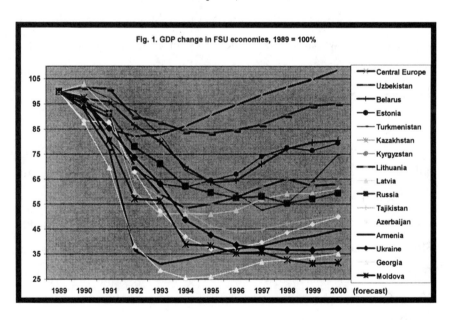

Fig. 1. GDP change in FSU economies, 1989 = 100%

Why has the reduction of output and incomes in FSU been so deep and so long? To what extent was this collapse caused by the initial conditions and circumstances, i.e. predetermined and hardly avoidable, and to what extent it was 'man made', i.e. became the result of poor economic policy choices? If it is the wrong economic policy that is mostly responsible for the collapse, future historians may refer to the FSU transition as the biggest "man made" economic disaster ever to happen.

The ubiquitous and virtually universal feeling is that "things went terribly wrong" and that with different policies it could have been possible to avoid most of the misfortunes that struck the former Soviet republics in the 1990s. After all, the majority other transition economies did better that the FSU states and it is difficult to accept the idea that the exceptional length and depth of recession in post Soviet states was predestined and inevitable.

However, when it comes to the discussion of particular policies, there is much less agreement among the scholars. The question of why the FSU had to pay a greater price for economic transition is answered differently by those who advocate shock therapy and those who support gradual piecemeal reforms. Shock therapists argue that much of the costs of the FSU reforms should be attributed to inconsistencies of policies followed, namely to the inability of the governments and the central banks to fight inflation in the first half of the 1990. On the other hand, the supporters of gradual transition state exactly the opposite, blaming the attempt to introduce conventional shock therapy package for all the disasters and misfortunes.

Quite a number of studies were undertaken with the intention to test whether fast liberalization and macro-stabilization pays off and finally leads to better performance.[1] To prove the point, the authors regressed output changes during transition on liberalization indices developed in De Melo et al. (1996) and by EBRD (published in its Transition Reports), inflation and different measures of initial conditions.

The conventional wisdom was probably summarized in the 1996 World Development Report (WDR) *From Plan to Market,* which basically stated that differences in economic performance were associated mostly with 'good and bad' policies, in particular with the progress in liberalization and macroeconomic stabilization. "Consistent policies, combining liberalization of markets, trade, and new business entry with reasonable price stability, can achieve a great deal even in countries lacking clear property rights and strong market institutions" – was one of the major conclusions of the WDR 1996.[2]

At a first glance, there seems to be a positive relationship between liberalization and performance (fig. 2). However, a more careful consideration reveals that the link is just the result of sharp difference in the magnitude of the recession in EE countries, as a group, and FSU states, also as a group (fig.2). Within these groups the correlation, if any, is much weaker, not to speak about China and Vietnam, which are outliers. The Chinese index of economic freedom (measured on a scale from 1 to 5 by the Heritage Foundation) was about the same in recent years as the Russian one, but the performance of the two countries differed markedly (fig. 3). Overall, attempts to link differences in output changes during transition to the cumulative liberalization index and to macro stabilization (rates of inflation) have not yielded any impressive results. Studies that tried to take into account a number of initial conditions (repressed inflation – monetary overhang before deregulation of prices, trade dependence, black market exchange rate premium, number of years under central planning, urbanization, over industrialization, and per capita income) found that in most cases liberalization becomes insignificant.[3]

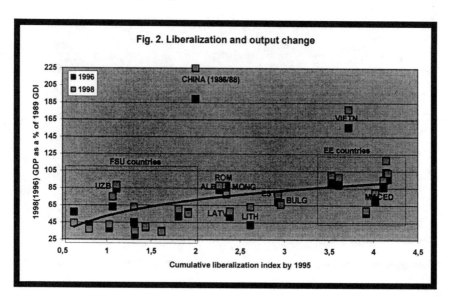

Fig. 2. Liberalization and output change

The alternative explanation of the collapse of output in the FSU accepted in this paper is that the speed of reform 'per se' (shock versus gradual transition) did not matter a great deal. The unique magnitude of the recession was caused primarily by three groups of factors. First, by greater distortions in the industrial structure and external trade patterns on the eve of the transition. Second, by the collapse of state and non-state institutions, which occurred in the late 1980s – early 1990s and which resulted in chaotic transformation through crisis management instead of organized and manageable transition. And third, by poor economic policies, which basically consisted of macroeconomic instability and import substitution, no matter whether the pursued reforms were gradual or radical.

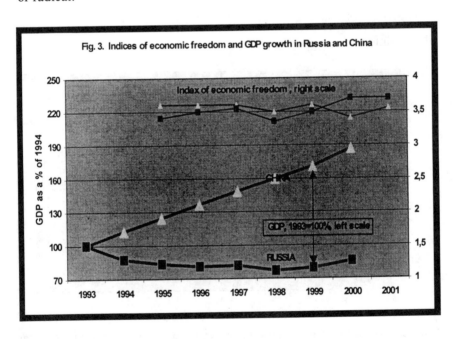

Fig. 3. Indices of economic freedom and GDP growth in Russia and China

In the first approximation, economic recession that occurred in the FSU states was associated with the need to reallocate resources in order to correct the industrial structure inherited from the centrally planned economy (CPE). These distortions include over-militarization and overindustrialization, perverted trade flows among former Soviet republics and Comecon countries, excessively large size and poor specialization of industrial enterprises and agricultural farms. In most cases these distortions were more pronounced than in Eastern Europe, not to mention China and Vietnam – the larger the distortions, the greater the reduction of output. The transformational recession, to put in economic terms, was caused by an adverse supply shock similar to the one experienced by Western countries after the oil price hikes in 1973 and 1979, and similar to post-war recessions caused by conversion of the defence industries.

The additional reason for the extreme depth of the transformational recession was associated with the institutional collapse – here differences between EE countries and FSU are striking. The adverse supply shock in this case came from the inability of the state to perform its traditional functions – to collect taxes and to constrain the shadow economy, to ensure property and contract rights and law and order in general. Naturally, poor ability to enforce rules and regulations did not create a business climate conducive to growth and resulted in increased costs for companies.

It is precisely this strong institutional framework that should be held responsible for both – for the success of gradual reforms in China and shock therapy in Vietnam, where strong authoritarian regimes were preserved and CPE institutions were not dismantled before new market institutions were created; and for the relative success of radical reforms in EE countries, especially in Central European countries, where strong democratic regimes and new market institutions emerged quickly. And it is precisely the collapse of the strong state and institutions that started in the USSR in the late 1980s and continued in the successor states in the 1990s that explains the extreme length, if not the extreme depth of the FSU transformational recession.

To put it differently, Gorbachev's reforms of 1985-91 failed not because they were gradual, but due to the weakening of the state institutional capacity leading to the inability of the government to control the flow of events. Similarly, Yeltsin reforms in Russia, as well as economic reforms in most other FSU states, were so costly not because of shock therapy, but due to the collapse of the institutions needed to enforce law and order and carry out manageable transition.

Finally, performance was of course affected by economic policy. Given the weak institutional capacity of the state, i.e. its poor ability to enforce its own regulations, economic policies could hardly be 'good'. Weak state institutions usually imply import substitution and populist macroeconomic policies (subsidies to noncompetitive industries, budget deficits resulting in high indebtedness and/or inflation, overvalued exchange rates), which have devastating impact on output. On the other hand, strong institutional capacity does not lead automatically to responsible economic policies. Examples range from the USSR before it collapsed (strong import substitution and periodic outbursts of open or hidden inflation) to such post Soviet states as Uzbekistan and Belarus, which seem to have stronger institutional potential than other FSU states, but do not demonstrate better policies (macroeconomic instability, for instance).

It turns out that the FSU transition model (with partial exemption of Uzbekistan, Belarus and Estonia) is based on a most misfortunate combination of unfavorable initial conditions, institutional degradation, and inefficient economic policies, such as macroeconomic populism and import substitution.

Notes
[1] Jeffrey D Sachs, "The Transition at Mid Decade", *Amer. Econom. Review*, 86:2, (1996): 128-133; Martha De Melo, Cevdet Denizer, and Alan Gelb, "Patterns of Transition From Plan to Market", *World Bank Econom. Review*, 3. (1996): 397-424; Stanley Fisher, Ratna Sahay, and Carlos A. Vegh, "Stabilization and Growth in the Transition Economies: The Early Experience", *Journal of Economic Perspectives,* 10.2, (1996): 45-66; A. Åslund, P. Boone, and S. Johnson, "How to Stabilize: Lessons from Post-Communist Countries" *Brookings Papers Econom. Activity*, 1, (1996): 217-313; P. Breton, D. Gros, and G. Vandille, "Output Decline and Recovery in the Transition Economies: Causes and Social Consequences", *Economics of Transition*, 5.1, (1997): 113-130; A. Berg, E. Borensztein, R. Sahay, and J. Zettelmeyer, "The Evolution of Output in Transition Economies: Explaining the Differences", IMF Working Paper, May 1999; Stanley Fisher, and Ratna Sahay, "The Transition Economies

After Ten Years", paper presented at the AEA meeting in Boston, (January 2000).
[2] *From Plan to Market. World Development Report*, (NY: Oxford U. Press, 1996) 142.
[3] Martha De Melo, Cavdet Denizer, Alan Gelb and Stoyan Tenev, "Circumstance and Choice: The Role of Initial Conditions and Policies in Transitions Economies", The World Bank, (October 1997); Berta Heybey, and Peter Murrell, "The Relationship between Economic Growth and the Speed of Liberalization During Transition", *Journal of Policy Reform*, 3.2, (1999); Gary Kruger, and Marek Ciolko, "A Note on Initial Conditions and Liberalization during Transition", *Journal of Comparative Economics*, 26.4, 618-34; V. Popov, "Shock Therapy versus Gradualism: The End of the Debate (Explaining the Magnitude of the Transformational Recession", *Comparative Economic Studies*, 42.1, (2000); V. Popov, "Reform Strategies and Economic Performance of Russia's Regions", *World Development* , (2001).

Causes of Failure: Why Russia's Oil Industry Did Not Attract Large Scale Foreign Investments?

Lilly A. Lo Manto, Undergraduate Student, York University

After the collapse of the Soviet Communism, many experts were expecting to see large-scale foreign direct investment (FDI)[1] into the Russian oil industry. However, the volume of FDI remained, until very recently, quite low. This essay will outline the causes of this failure. Factors such as fluctuations of the world oil market, the rate of Russia's capital depreciation and the impact of economic geography will be discussed. The main focus of the paper is on the role of the federal government and oil industry executives in the privatization process and the relations between them. Conflicts of interests over resource rents between the centre and the periphery, as well as the inability of the newly reconstructed federal government to create secure and transparent tax and legal frameworks fostered financial instability that dispelled any foreign investment incentives. Meanwhile, failed governance led to the transfer of decision-making power to the economic elite whose short-term interest in wealth accumulation precluded the involvement of foreign investment.

In the early 1990s, the West had high hopes for the role FDI would play in Russia's fiscal recovery, transition to a market system and reintegration into the world economy.[2] Working closely with state agencies, foreign oil majors would introduce universal standards, encourage local research and development, and offer scientific and technical training[3] – all of which the state energy complex required in order to function and develop.[4] Moreover, by increasing production capacity, providing training and employment, and "introduce[ing] a demonstration effect to domestic producers regarding world standards in terms of marketing, production, and service provision",[5] FDI would give Western firms a direct stake in the success of the reform process.[6] Major Western multinationals were particularly attracted by the potential of Russia's untapped hydrocarbon reserves, so as to meet the energy demands of the European and rapidly growing Asian markets.[7] Indeed, high earnings could be garnered from Russia's oil resources, which ranked second in proven recoverable reserves[8] and fed seventeen percent of the world's crude oil consumption.[9] Additional investment incentives included cost reductions, through access to a low-cost but highly skilled labour force and lax environmental production standards.[10]

From the outset, however, three factors limited the participation of foreign investment in the Russian oil sector: the country's economic geography, the volatility of the international oil market, and the rate of Russia's inherited capital depreciation. Indeed, "severity of climate, distance (including the location of population as compared to natural resources) and the preponderance of costly land transport over cheap sea transport"[11] served to amplify the costs of Russian oil production. Furthermore, plentiful oil supplies led to a decline in world oil prices in the 1990s.[12] In fact, abundant supplies and dwindling prices created challenges for petroleum suppliers who were forced to "focus their efforts on reducing cost and improving productivity, effectively using new technology and building on their core competencies and competitive advantage".[13] Such tasks were difficult to accomplish in Russia, considering the country's declining capital stock[14] inherited from its previous regime whose penchant for water-injection technology, while boosting the rate of short-term extraction, increased damage to oil wells, thus effectively limiting long-term productive capacity.[15]

Understanding the policies of the former Soviet Union concerning both oil production and foreign investment is, as C.H. McMillan maintains, necessary for understanding the role played by FDI in Russia's emerging petroleum sector in the 1990s.[16] In the Communist era, the oil industry was among the most important productive sectors,[17] providing the main source of foreign currency earnings that were used to finance the imports of consumer goods, equipment and machinery.[18] However, accounting standards were primitive, management was insensitive to costs, services were provided on poorly defined contractual bases, and deliveries were made to traditional customers regardless of ability to pay or cost considerations.[19] Moreover, by the end of 1985, the fall in world oil prices seriously undermined the regime's external financial position. As the volume of oil production and export dropped, Soviet policy-makers considered the application of foreign technology, through FDIs, as a viable method of reversing these downward turns.[20] Championed by Communist Party General, Mikhail Gorbachev, this approach fostered government policies of openness and facilitated economic reforms.

It is important to note that Gorbachev's reforms, known as 'Perestroika', "amounted to no less than a complete reversal of a strong ideologically motivated aversion to Western capital",[21] encouraging the formation of cooperatives, small businesses and joint ventures (JVs)[22]. Indeed, several new laws, adopted in early January 1987, reopened the Soviet economy, for the first time since the 1920s, to limited forms of foreign equity investment by capitalist firms. Three years later, the government permitted the establishment of wholly foreign-owned companies in the form of branches or subsidiaries, and, less than six months before the dissolution of the USSR, the-newly elected President of the Russian Federation, Boris Yeltsin, signed a comprehensive foreign investment law that would survive the Soviet Union's collapse.[23] Although the USSR did experience an increase in foreign investment,[24] in the second half of the 1980s, such growth was modest. In addition to being affected by the confusing regulatory environment for FDI, investors were leery to invest in a climate of political and economic turmoil characteristic of the Soviet Union's final years.[25] In the end, Gorbachev's endeavours to create 'organic links' to the global market mostly fostered foreign enclaves, separate from the national economy.[26]

Indeed, in 1992, when Boris Yeltsin, President of the newly independent Russian Federation, asked for decree powers, noting that economic reforms were "impossible to carry out without sufficiently firm measures by the entire system of executive power",[27] there were little more than two thousand foreign investment projects in Russia.[28] In the same year, the Ministry of Fuel and Energy (MINTOP) was established. Charged with the legal and administrative regulation of the fuel and energy complex, the new federal agency was to secure jurisdiction over the newly privatized companies and assure the flow of taxation revenue to the central treasury[29]. Nonetheless, by the autumn of the same year, following the dissolution of Soviet ministries, there was a marked shift in political control from the centre to the periphery.[30] Together, enterprises and organs of local administration began to assert their own sovereignty, as regional governments became active promoters of local oil enterprises, being interested in the collection of taxes.[31] Power struggles between Moscow and the republics ensued over the regulation of high profit-earning sectors. Such tensions stymied Russia's emerging federalism and served as the political backdrop to the privatization process.[32]

Guided by the ideology of liberal market capitalism,[33] the first phase of Russia's privatization, was aimed at fostering a more open economy.[34] President Yeltsin stated in June 1992: "We hope to accommodate foreign investment to the tune of hundreds of billions of dollars".[35] However, the government's rather lax monetary policy, characterized by the extensive financing of bankrupt ventures and the printing of large amounts of roubles led to serious financial instability.[36] The state's inability to create an institutional structure for a market economy was further exemplified by the results of the first privatization auctions, where competitions to privatize low stock market value state enterprises[37] through the use of vouchers[38] invariably turned out to be "management-employee buy-out program[s]".[39] Despite the presidential decree of November 1992 that stipulated the state's majority ownership rights, in the following year the privatization of the Russian oil industry was typified by governmental passivity.[40] Top Russian oil majors began to affirm their control through the minority stakes the state put up for sale, while foreigners were only permitted to purchase up to fifteen percent of a stock in a Russian petroleum company.[41] Consequently, managers of local enterprises and regional government leaders began to take over assets in the oil industry,[42] with no major external participation.[43] Indeed, by the end of 1993, there had not been a single major foreign investment in the industry, since the Soviet Union's collapse, leading experts such as McMillan to conclude: "a foreign investment boom in Russia is not just not around the corner".[44]

In mid-1994, as power overwhelmingly flowed to the hands of the managerial elite, what Daniel J. McCarthy et al. term as the 'nomenklatura' stage of privatization[45] effectively began. For the following three years, the official governmental goal was to help create funds for the restructuring of newly privatized Russian enterprises.[46] In truth, revenues earned from the piecemeal cash privatization of valuable firms engaged in the production of raw materials and utilities were used to finance growing federal budget deficits.[47] Scholars such as Allen C.

Lynch blame the political and administrative sphere for Russia's prolonged economic decline in the 1990s.[48] This period was marked by the existence of a political regime built around the presidency and the prime minister[49] that lacked the necessary state apparatus for effective taxation – essential for fostering a sound investment climate.[50] Russia's tax system, largely inherited from Soviet times, was characterized by the proliferation of tax offsets and the growth of a web of tax exemptions and deferrals granted by various levels of government[51]. Although Yeltsin's government maintained the Soviet tradition of subsidizing the industrial sector via the revenues garnered from resource-rich areas, Susan L. Clark and David R. Graham note that the "unwillingness of people in certain areas of Russia and certain individual enterprises to subsidize the federal government" amounted to a virtual tax revolt.[52] Indeed, during this period, oil producers resisted paying their full share of taxes.[53] Furthermore, the frequent changes in the tax system not only impeded domestic planning and compliance – fostering "powerful incentives to evade taxes",[54] – but also served to undermine financial incentives established to attract foreign investment.[55] By the end of 1996, total tax concessions amounted to over seven percent of GDP.[56] The state's inability to raise sufficient tax revenue hindered the government capacity to regulate of the macro-economy and to honour domestic and foreign fiduciary obligations.[57] The inevitable outcome was a weak central state that permitted "its leaders to pass over control of parts of the economy to private interests".[58]

The desire to use privatization as an alternative to revenue collection acted as an incentive for such a reversal of power and culminated in the program that came to be known as 'loans-for-shares'.[59] In this scheme, adopted by presidential decree on 31 August 1995,[60] Russian investors would take over for a specified period a part of the government's share in trust management, in exchange for supplying the state with credit.[61] If the state could not repay, the lender would then auction off the stock collateral to the highest bidder, keep a fraction of the proceeds equivalent to the value of the loan, and return remaining revenue to the government.[62] A consortium of new Russian banks participated as lending parties. Since the government was consistently unable to make the credit repayments, the banks seized the opportunity to organize auctions to their own financial advantage,[63] involving "predetermined transfers to friends and insiders, with only a fig leaf of an auction or market sale".[64] Indeed, as Marshall I. Goldman noted, rarely did more than one bidder materialize. Each of the bidders represented an organization associated with the bank conducting the auction, while all other bidders, even if they offered a higher price, were disqualified on some or other technicality. Ultimately, the state was the invariable loser, receiving only a fraction more than the original price of the loans.[65]

The oil sector was not an exception to this, but rather its perfect example. By 1996, a major reconstruction of the industry had taken place whereby the government was no longer the majority owner in many holding companies.[66] One such entity was Russia's second largest oil corporation, YuKOS.[67] On 8 December 1995, the Menatep bank initiated an investment 'loans-for-shares' auction, through which it procured 78% of YuKOS shares through an intermediary company named Luguna. The only other bidder permitted to participate was Reagent, another Menatep-sponsored company.[68] Both Luguna and Reagent were formed mere days before the auction, with the bank's financial backing. The following year, in order to pay off a two trillion-rouble wage and tax debt,[69] Menatep initiated, with the government's participation, a state-shares auction.[70] At which time, the bank effectively decreased its exposure but retained both direct and indirect control of ninety-four percent of YuKOS shares. However, the state's revenue from the auction was insignificant, for, as Valery Kryukov and Arild Moe write, "the conditions for the competition were 160 million dollars plus an investment program of 200 million dollars, approximately the same amount stipulated in the conditions for the loans-for-shares auction a year earlier".[71]

Ultimately, in order to solidify their power and wealth,[72] large conglomerates known as financial and industrial groups (FIGs), mainly controlled by former Communist party functionaries put in charge of managing state oil enterprises, would set aside a portion of the government's oil assets for privatization while maintaining positions as executive officers and major stockholders in newly formed petroleum companies.[73] Ken I. Kim and Anna Yelkina estimate that "more than seventy percent of the shares of privatized companies wound up in the hands of such individuals",[74] who considered themselves sovereign and capable of pursing a hegemonic role within the industry.[75] FIGs formed interest lobbies which, through insider managerial collusion, ensured the provision of collective state benefits,[76] in the form of discriminatory transfer pricing, share swaps within holding companies, restricted access to shareholder meetings, and share dilution,[77] and thus preserved control, avoided outside ownership[78] and invariably circumscribed the entry of FDI into the Russian oil sector.

It is also very important to note the government's inadequate attention to designing legislative and contractual frameworks[79] through the development of production sharing agreements (PSAs).[80] Fundamentally, the adoption of PSAs would have attracted FDI by promoting: 1) investor shares of exportable production; 2) investors' access to pipelines; 3) local regulations; and 4) tax calculations.[81] Ultimately, the implementation of PSAs would have granted foreign investors equality of interests in the sharing of output and revenue,[82] while insulating them from the risks of changing legislation and tax rates.[83] Yeltsin struggled to convince the Duma to formalize the rules governing PSAs in Russia,[84] but "conservative and nationalist opposition to the agreement...blocked their path at almost every turn".[85] Nevertheless, in July 1997, Yeltsin signed one of the key pieces of legislation required for the implementation of PSAs. In the same year, confronted with serious budget deficits, Yeltsin lifted not only the restriction on the sale of oil assets but also the fifteen percent legal limit of shares that foreigners could own.[86] Consequently, foreign investors came to possess more than twenty percent of share capital in the Russian oil giant LUKoil and a further fifteen percent planned investment tender, both of which exceeded the eight percent stock required for placement on the board of directors.[87] In addition, 'case-by-case' privatization was introduced requiring sales to be carried out under the control of the Russian State Property Ministry (GKI), observing the principles of publicity and openness.[88] The financial crisis of 1998[89] pushed Yeltsin to make a series of declarations on protecting minority shareholder rights, abolishing tax offsets, and promising tax reforms – all of which would provide a friendlier climate[90] for FDI, albeit with increased state involvement and intervention in the economic arena.[91]

However, these measures could not offset the adverse economic effects of explicit and tacit collusion practiced between the managerial and state elites throughout the 1990s.[92] In general, collusion between Russian political and economic actors was to be expected, for, as Kathryn Stoner-Weiss explains: "the more highly concentrated (in terms of assets, labour, and productive output) a region's economy is in a particular economic sector (oil...for example), the more consensus there is between political and economic elites regarding developmental goals".[93] But, in this case, long-standing capital reinvestment objectives were sacrificed for immediate personal financial gains – actions that invariably promoted the development of corruption networks.[94] Such associations facilitated both the laundering of illegal profits made from oil smuggling and investment of legal revenues overseas in order to avoid domestic taxation and obtain lucrative investment opportunities.[95] In particular, Russia's oil industry engaged in illegal capital transfers abroad that, according to the World Bank (WB), exceeded the total volume of capital flowing into the country.[96] In fact, conservative WB estimates show that, from 1993 to 1997, 88.7 billion dollars fled Russia.[97] Ultimately, the general "dearth of foreign capital investment" that characterized the state of Russia's economy throughout the 1990s,[98] was a result of the state's failure to attract mass foreign ventures.[99] Although FDI was sectorialized, with most funds going to the energy sector,[100] oil production still decreased from eleven million to under seven million barrels per day: apart from Saudi Arabia, an amount equivalent to the total output of any other member of the Organization of Petroleum Exporting Countries (OPEC)103.[101] In fact, foreign investment in Russia was "essentially 'enclave' investment that [did] not produce a general transformation in national economic fortunes but creat[ed] distortions in economic structure similar to those produced in a shift to dependency", suggesting that FDI actually remained stagnant throughout the so-called post-communist economic transformation. By the end of 1998, despite its privatization blitz, Russia occupied but a peripheral position in the global economy, reduced to a raw material supplier.[102]

In conclusion, despite promising revenue possibilities, from 1990 to 1998, foreign investment did not play a significant role in shaping the post-Communist oil sector. The period's political instability, characterized by opaque rule of law, a weak taxation system, bureaucratic infighting, macroeconomic instability and collusion practiced amongst and between economic and state elite, served as major impediments against any significant FDI. Invariably the inhospitable investment environment limited the flow of foreign capital and technology required to modernize the Russian economy.

Notes

[1] As defined by Valdas Samonis, in this essay, foreign investment will be understood as a process of acquiring a country's productive assets and/or adding to its capital stock, through two forms, portfolio or direct. The former, gives the investor no direct control over assets and management, the latter, on the other hand, provides the investor with such control. Valdas Samonis, *Foreign Investment in the East: Modelling the Experience* (New York: Nova Science, 1995) 2.

[2] C.H. McMillan, "Foreign Investment in Russia: Soviet Legacies and Post-Soviet Prospects," *Occasional Paper* n 5 (1994): 6.

[3] Imle Jr 268. FDI was seen as a major factor promoting the world's economic development because it provided the most effective channel for the transfer of marketing, technological and organizational skills. Samonis 3.

[4] Lane, *introduction* 7.

[5] Kathryn Stoner-Weiss, "Foreign Direct Investment and Democratic Development in the Russian Provinces: A Preliminary Analysis," *Policy Studies Journal* 28.2 (2000): 96.

[6] McMillan 5.

[7] Jennifer Nicoud and Matthew J. Sagers, "Development of the East Siberian Gas Field and Pipeline to China: A Research Communication," *Post-Soviet Geography and Economics* 38.5 (1997): 291. By 2020, crude oil demand is estimated to exceed 115 million barrels per day, of which about 60 million barrels per day will be consumed by countries now part of the non-industrialized world. John F. Imle Jr, "Multinationals and the New World of Energy Development: A Corporate Perspective," *Journal of International Affairs* 53.1 (1999): 266.

[8] David Lane, introduction, *The Political Economy of Russian Oil*, ed. David Lane, (New York: Rowman & Littlefield, 1999) 2. As to the actual figures there are discrepancies in the literature: For example, while David Lane avers that Russia ranked second in proven recoverable oil reserves, Fiona Hill states that

Russia is also behind the United States, ranking her third at just over 7 million barrels per day. Fiona Hill, "Russia: the 21ˢᵗ Century's Energy Superpower?" *Brookings Review* 20.2 (2002): 30.

[9] Allen C. Lynch, "Roots of Russia's Economic Dilemmas: Liberal Economics and Illiberal Geography," *Europe-Asia Studies* 54.1 (2002): 32.

[10] Samonis 5.

[11] Lynch 31, 39.

[12] Susan L. Clark and David R. Graham, "The Russian Federation's Fight for Survival," *ORBIS* 39.3 (1995): 337.

[13] According the World Oil Trends, in 1993, the price of oil was at a twenty-year low in real terms. "World Oil Trends Defined in Study by Arthur Anderson and CERA," *Hydrocarbon Processing* 73.3 (1994): 1.

[14] In 1995, the average age of industrial equipment was 14.1 years, and twenty-three percent of industrial capital stock was older than twenty years. Lynch 33.

[15] Marshall I. Goldman, "Russian Energy: A Blessing and a Curse," *Journal of International Affairs* 53.1 (1999): 75.

[16] There were substantial capital inflows, before the 1917 revolution, in the form of portfolio investment: the financing of industrial development projects through long-term bonds guaranteed by the Tsarist regime. McMillan 5, 13.

[17] Valery Kryukov and Arild Moe, "Banks and the Financial Sector," *The Political Economy of Russian Oil*, ed. David Lane, (New York: Rowman & Littlefield, 1999) 61.

[18] Lane, *introduction* 1.

[19] Vladimir Caplik and Ben Slay, "Natural Monopoly Regulation and Competition Policy in Russia," *Antitrust Bulletin* 43.1 (1998): 2

[20] McMillan 13-14.

[21] Samonis 6.

[22] Daniel J. McCarthy et al., "Russia's Retreat to Statization and the Implications for Business," *Journal of World Business* 35.3 (2000): 258. Samonis defines Joint Equity Ventures as the "pooling of broadly defined capital assets by at least two firms, called parents or partners, in order to create a separate legal entity pursuing business activities in which partners actively participate as decision makers" Samonis 6. The Law of the State Enterprise of 30 June 1987 confirmed the participation of Soviet enterprises in JVs. McMillan 15.

[23] The following day, the Soviet government passed a new foreign investment law, so as to consolidate the existing foreign investment regulations that had been issued in 1987. McMillan 5, 14-15, 21, 37.

[24] Samonis 4.

[25] McMillan 36, 41.

[26] Samonis 1, 32.

[27] Neil Robinson, "The Economy and the Prospects for Anti-Democratic Development in Russia," *Europe-Asia Studies* 52.8 (2000): 1406.

[28] McMillan 40.

[29] David Lane and Iskander Seifulmulukov, "Structure and Ownership," *The Political Economy of Russian Oil*, ed. David Lane, (New York: Rowman & Littlefield, 1999) 16, 18.

[30] Lane, *introduction* 4.

[31] Stoner-Weiss 100.

[32] McMillan 22

[33] Lane, *Structure* 42

[34] McCarthy et al. 259.

[35] Made during a state visit to the United States (US). McMillan 42.

[36] Including rampant hyperinflation, considerable capital flight, rapidly decreasing output and rising unemployment. Marcella Mulino, "On the Determinants of Capital Flight from Russia," *Atlantic Economic Journal* 30.2 (2002): 153.

[37] Trevor Buck et al. "Exporting Activity in Transnational Economies: An Enterprise-Level Study," *Journal of Development Studies* 37.2 (2000): 49.

[38] The first phase of privatization, known as "voucher privatization", began in early 1993, and consisted of issuing vouchers representing ownership shares in enterprises and organizations that were formally owned by the state. McCarthy et al. 260. The vouchers could be used to bid for and buy shares in privatization auctions, before the expiration date of 1 July 1994. Ken I. Kim and Anna Yelkina, "Privatization in Russia: its Past, Present, and Future," *SAM Advanced Management Journal* 68.1 (2003): 15.

[39] Mulino 156.

[40] Lane, *Structure* 23.

[41] Kryukov 65, 68.

[42] Lane, *introduction* 5.

[43] Kryukov 68.

[44] McMillan 49, 51.

[45] McCarthy et al describe this period as being driven by "the excesses of inept and corrupt members of the Yeltsin's government and well-placed business people". 257

[46] McCarthy et al. 262

[47] Kim 16.

[48] Lynch 37.

[49] Robinson 1406.

[50] Mulino 155.

[51] The term 'war of laws' typifies this behaviour, which describes the struggle between Moscow and the republics as different levels of government attempted to affirm their own jurisdiction by issuing conflicting regulations. McMillan 22.

[52] Clark 340.

[53] Goldman 83.

[54] Mulino 161.

[55] McMillan 26.

[56] Mulino 162.

[57] Lynch 38.

[58] Robinson 1405.

[59] Goldman 77.

[60] The 'loans-for-shares' plan was first announced by presidential decree no. 478 on 11 May 1995. Kim 17.

[61] Kryukov 62.

[62] Goldman 78.

[63] Robinson 1404.

[64] Richard E. Ericson, "Does Russia Have a 'Market Economy'?" *East European Politics and Societies* 15.1 (2001): 308.

[65] Goldman 78.

[66] Lane, *Structure* 18.

[67] Peter Rutland, "Banks Continue to Dispute YuKOS Auction," *Analytical Briefs* i2789 (1995) 5 Sept. 2003 <http://archive.tol.cz/omri/resultindex.php3> . At the time, in terms of total recoverable and proven oil reserves, YuKOS was the top Russian oil company with a total of 2.1 billion tonnes of recoverable oil

resources. David Lane and Iskander Seifulmulukov, "Company Profiles: YuKOS," *The Political Economy of Russian Oil*, ed. David Lane, (New York: Rowman & Littlefield, 1999) 114.

[68] Guaranteed by Menatep, Luguna offered 150 million dollars for a thirty-three percent stake in the investment auction. In addition, for a forty-five percent stake, the company provided a credit of 159 million dollars guaranteed by the Menatep, Tokobank, and Stolichnyi banks. Natalia Gurushina, "Menatep Gains Control of YuKOS," *Analytical Briefs* i2640 (1995) 5 Sept. 2003 <http://archive.tol.cz/omri/resultindex.php3>.

[69] Peter Rutland, "Legal Challenge to Loan/Share Auctions," *Analytical Briefs* i5987 (1996) 5 Sept. 2003 <http://archive.tol.cz/omri/resultindex.php3?pattern=yukos&rows=10&page=2>

[70] The Finance Ministry, the State Property Committee, and the Federal Property Fund approved Menatep's plans. Natalia Gurushina, "Menatep to Sell Stakes in YuKOS," *Analytical Briefs* i22033 (1996) 5 Sept. 2003 <http://archive.tol.cz/omri/resultindex.php3?pattern=yukos&rows=10&page=2.

[71] Kryukov 65.

[72] McCarthy et al. 265.

[73] A perfect example is Vagit Alekperov, the acting minister of the former Soviet Fuel and Energy Ministry, who amassed lucrative properties, including oil fields and refineries, into what became LUKoil. He and other new owners are on Forbe's list of billionaires, despite their net assets, before the privatization process, amounting to less than fifty thousand dollars. Goldman 77.

[74] Kim 16.

[75] Lane, *Structure* 41-42.

[76] Stoner-Weiss 49.

[77] Mulino 157.

[78] Buck et al. 49. Foreign oil multinationals adversely affected include: Amoco, Bechtel Energy Resource, BHP Petroleum of Australia, Elf Aquitaine, Exxon, Gulg Canada Resources, Norsk Hydor, Pennsopil and Texaco. Goldman 80-81.

[79] Mulino 157

[80] For the past thirty years, PSAs have been used all over the world, allowing both the state and the foreign investor to negotiate the terms of the contract, while holding the state liable should it breach the established agreement. "Russia: Oil and Gas," *Energy Division*, ed. Rachel Halpem. April 2002. International Trade Administration. 20 Sept. 2003: <http://www.ita.doc.gov/td/energy/ruso&g.html>.

[81] Geoffrey Townsend, "Russia – Why so long to establish a Production Sharing Regime?" *WorldPower Interim* Oct 2001: 24-25.

[82] Goldman 79.

[83] Before the existence of PSA legislation in Russia, initial JV arrangements did not adequately protect the interests of foreign investors against arbitrary changes in conditions and demands for authorities at various levels of government, leading many JVs to suffer substantial loses. Consequently, Western oil companies expressed a strong preference to operate with the security of PSAs. David G. Victor and Nadejda M. Victor, "Axis of Oil?" *Foreign Affairs* 82.2 (2003): 55-66.

[84] Goldman 80.

[85] "Duma is Working on a Second List for PSAs," *Alexander's Gas and Oil Connections News & Trends: CIS/Russia* 2.16 (1997) 5 Sept. 2003 <http://www.gasandoil.com/goc/news/ntr72303.htm>.

[86] However, oil companies were permitted to fix a ceiling limiting foreign investment. Lane, *Structure* 35-36.

[87] Lane, *Structure* 30.

[88] The government arranged cash auctions, in order to sell stakes in the following six oil corporations: Komi TEK, Norsi-Oil, Siberail-Ural Petro-Gas-Chemical Company, Tyumen Oil Company, Vostochanaya Neftyanaya Kompaniya, and Vostsibneftgazm. Kim 18.

[89] Robinson describes the 1998 financial crisis as: "the government could no longer defend the rouble and had to announce a moratorium on the payment of foreign commercial debts and a freeze on domestic debt repayments due to a combination of poor state revenue, falling oil prices, government instability, knock-on effects from the crisis on Asian markets, lack of liquidity in the banking sector and intransigence from the Duma and the IMF". 1403-1404.

[90] Homi Kharas et al. "An Analysis of Russia's 1998 Meltdown: Fundamentals and Market Signals," *Brookings Papers on Economic Activity* 1 (2001): 8.

[91] McCarthy et al. 265.

[92] McCarthy et al. point out Menatep as one of the most flagrant examples of such a situation: a major conglomerate with major holdings in banks, enterprises and natural resources. 263.

[93] Stoner-Weiss 97-98.

[94] Heiko Pleines, "Corruption and Crime in the Russian Oil Industry," *The Political Economy of Russian Oil*, ed. David Lane, (New York: Rowman &

Littlefield, 1999) 101. In this essay, corruption is defined as "the use of public position and resources for private gain". Ericson 304.

[95] Pleines 104.

[96] Robinson explains that it is highly plausible that a large portion of what passed for foreign portfolio investment was actually the return of illegally exported Russian capital. 1414-1415.

[97] McCarthy et al. 264.

[98] Lynch 31. Between 1989 and 1995, the cumulative FDI inflow per capita into Russia was at U.S. $21 billion. Stoner-Weiss 96. Only in 1997, did foreign investment provide more than three percent of capital investment. Robinson 1402.

[99] Kim 18.

[100] Robinson 1400.

[101] Hydrocarbon 1. Production fell by 7.0 percent in 1990, 10.7 percent in 1991, 14.2 percent in 1992, 13.1 percent in 1993, 8.2 percent in 1994, 2.9 percent in 1995, and 1.8 percent on 1996. Matthew J. Sagers, "Turnaround in Russian Oil Production in 1997," *Post-Soviet Geography and Economics* 38.8 (1997): 499.

[102] Robinson 1400, 1402.

Section 4

Russia in the World

Canada-Russia Relations: A Canadian View
Honourable Bill Graham, Minister of Foreign Affairs of Canada

Je vous remercie de votre invitation à prendre part à cette conférence. En tant que Torontois et francophile, vous comprendrez que j'ai une affection particulière pour le Collège Glendon, une institution construite à partir de deux idéaux qui me sont chers, soit le bilinguisme et le biculturalisme.

Je dois avouer que le fait de discuter de l'état actuel des relations canado-russes me place devant un certain dilemme. Normalement, dans ces occasions, j'aime débuter par une citation marquante sur la question dont nous sommes saisis. Il n'y a pas si longtemps, j'aurais pu me présenter devant vous en citant Winston Churchill, qui comparait la Russie à « une devinette enveloppée dans un mystère à l'intérieur d'une énigme ». En 2002 toutefois, il appert que les citations pertinentes sur la Russie se montrent difficiles à trouver, en raison du rythme fulgurant auquel des changements remarquables se sont produits dans ce pays. Ainsi donc, les grands esprits et les spécialistes ne semblent pas encore avoir pu prendre la pleine mesure de ces changements, du moins pas assez pour produire des phrases dignes de faire l'objet de citations « lumineuses » ou « éblouissantes ».

Je débuterai donc aujourd'hui par une observation – c'est-à-dire que, en contraste avec les autres enjeux importants qui sont ces jours-ci à l'ordre du jour international, notre relation avec la Russie se caractérise surtout par des possibilités et des développements que je n'hésite pas à qualifier d'essentiellement positifs. En réalité, d'un point de vue canadien, les crises actuelles de l'Iraq et de la Corée du Nord mettent en évidence l'évolution remarquable de notre perception du rôle de la Russie dans le monde. En termes plus directs, nous voyons la Russie comme faisant non pas partie du problème, mais plutôt, et de plus en plus, comme étant une partie de la solution dans les affaires mondiales.

Aujourd'hui, avec d'autres pays du monde, le Canada œuvre de concert avec la Russie afin d'apporter des solutions pacifiques et durables aux défis posés par l'Iraq et la Corée du Nord. Et il ne fait aucun doute à mes yeux que cette coopération entre nos pays aidera à faire face aux autres crises qui surgiront dans l'avenir. Donc, si nous avons pu participer et assister aux progrès des relations canado-russes au cours des deux dernières décennies, je souhaite aujourd'hui que nous abordions ensemble ces réalisations sous l'angle des progrès que nous sommes appelés à accomplir ensemble dans les années à venir.

Au risque de retomber dans le rôle dévolu par mon ancienne vie de professeur, permettez-moi d'aborder d'entrée de jeu le contexte historique dans lequel les relations canado-russes se sont développées, tout en relevant quelques-uns des grands thèmes qui en ont découlé.

Depuis que les gouvernements canadien et russe ont commencé à s'intéresser l'un à l'autre au début du XXe siècle, les relations entre nos deux pays se sont surtout caractérisées par deux dimensions distinctes.

L'une d'elles découlait de la dimension mondiale de la sécurité internationale où, pour des motifs idéologiques sinon militaires, la Russie, plus souvent qu'autrement, représentait un sujet principal de préoccupation pour le Canada et ses alliés. L'autre dimension était notre dimension bilatérale, où les flux migratoires et les contacts sportifs, de même que les territoires nordiques qui font de nous des voisins, permettaient de faire entendre une tonalité plus positive.

Il est vrai que l'alignement géopolitique de l'après-Deuxième Guerre mondiale a placé le Canada et la Russie dans des camps opposés pendant plusieurs décennies. Cependant, une caractéristique a néanmoins distingué le Canada des autres pays occidentaux pendant cette période : en effet, nos deux pays ont pu tout de même travailler ensemble, et combler les fossés politique et idéologique, notamment par la coopération mutuelle dans des domaines d'intérêt commun.

Ainsi, en dépit de la guerre froide, cette tendance distinguant le Canada a pu se manifester dès la visite en Union soviétique, en 1956, du secrétaire d'État aux Affaires extérieures, Lester B. Pearson. Il vaut certes la peine de souligner que c'était là une première visite en URSS de la part d'un ministre des Affaires étrangères d'un pays de l'OTAN (Organisation du Traité de l'Atlantique Nord). Le Canada a aussi été, dès les années 1960, le premier pays occidental à signer d'importants accords de ventes de céréales avec l'Union soviétique. De plus, nous avons été le premier pays de l'OTAN à avoir rompu un boycott imposé au moment de la crise tchécoslovaque, et ce, en invitant au Canada le ministre soviétique des Affaires étrangères Andreï Gromyko.

La différence canadienne s'est encore exprimée au moment de la visite officielle de Pierre Elliott Trudeau en Union soviétique en 1971, ainsi que lors de plusieurs autres visites ministérielles, y compris le voyage en Sibérie en 1971 de Jean Chrétien, qui était alors ministre des Affaires indiennes. Cette visite a d'ailleurs eu des incidences significatives à long terme, car elle a permis de désigner la coopération dans l'Arctique et dans le Nord comme l'un des défis communs pouvant rapprocher nos deux pays, et ce « en dépit », selon le langage de l'époque, « de divergences idéologiques ».

La disposition du Canada à développer des liens de coopération avec l'Union soviétique s'est avérée encore plus évidente avec l'arrivée au pouvoir de Mikhaïl Gorbatchev, qui a d'ailleurs eu lieu très peu de temps après sa visite mémorable au Canada. À la veille des bouleversements qui ont secoué l'Europe de l'Est en 1989, la visite officielle du premier ministre du Canada en Union soviétique en novembre de cette même année a également permis aux relations entre nos deux pays de franchir une nouvelle étape, tout en donnant le ton pour les années à venir. Ainsi, lorsque la Russie a décidé de se défaire du dogme communiste et de ses structures d'économie dirigiste, bon nombre de Canadiens ont acquis la conviction que la nouvelle Russie méritait notre appui pour traverser la période de transition qui l'attendait. Le programme d'assistance technique de l'Agence canadienne de développement international [ACDI] a d'ailleurs fourni beaucoup d'aide à cette fin, particulièrement pour renforcer la sphère qu'on appelle aujourd'hui la société civile, qui est essentielle à la vitalité de toute société démocratique.

In the past decade, the Canada-Russia relationship has grown far beyond the relatively narrow intergovernmental dimensions that had characterized our relations with the U.S.S.R. On the political side, senior officials from both countries have annual meetings on strategic stability that now cover the whole range of international security and disarmament issues. On the economic side, we have the Intergovernmental Economic Commission, first convened in 1995, which is an industry-led bilateral forum aiming to foster trade, investment and the transfer of technology. Although it is called intergovernmental, this Commission in fact goes beyond strictly intergovernmental relations into broader areas of trade and investment.

Both the Canadian and Russian governments are keen to heighten the economic dimension of our bilateral relationship to match the level of our political ties. The relatively undeveloped level of business familiarity and comfort is partly a function of the fact that, until recently, Canada has not had a large Russian-speaking community. However, there has been an enormous increase in the Russian-speaking community over the past decade in places such as Toronto – a fact reflected by the recent opening of a Russian Consulate-General in this city. This development should improve matters by bridging the language gap, promoting business contacts, and improving mutual knowledge. The

Intergovernmental Economic Commission will be important in taking advantage of this change, so that Canadian and Russian business communities will be brought closer together.

Building a climate of investor confidence and stability will also be helped by the structural reforms that President Putin and his team are carrying out, including their drive to bring Russia into the WTO. But already there are successes reflected in the growth of high level bilateral contacts, including a strong personal relationship between Russian and Canadian leaders, that began with President Putin's visit here in December 2000. And as for the Team Canada mission to Moscow in February 2002, while its economic impact will be measured more precisely in a year or two, its impact can already be felt in terms of our perception of Russia as a dynamic business environment.

At the multilateral level, Canada took on the goal of integrating Russia into the G7 during the Halifax Summit, in 1995; and at the Kananaskis Summit, in 2002, the process concluded with a decision to have Russia assume the G8 presidency and host the Summit in 2006. Canada has also promoted a NATO-Russia relationship that would better reflect new realities; and, in fact, the creation of the NATO-Russia Council last year also stems from a Canadian initiative.

On every level, I can say that relations between Russia and Canada have never been as good as they are at present. I could give you a long list of examples in support of this claim, but I can also attest to it through my own experience as Chair of the House of Commons Committee on Foreign Affairs, and now as Minister of Foreign Affairs. Following my visit to Moscow last November, I can assure you that relations with my Russian colleagues are excellent, and that the openness and quality of our dialogue leaves nothing to be desired.

And beyond the intergovernmental level, Canadian provinces, municipalities, universities and other organizations have established a growing network of relations with their Russian counterparts, opening up contacts in the commercial, cultural and academic spheres.

Canada and Russia are also well-placed to be partners in the global community. We are working together on many issues such as the International Criminal Court, and the prevention of an arms race in outer space; and a central element of our international security relationship with Russia will come through our participation in the G8 Global Partnership Against the Spread of Weapons and Materials of Mass Destruction. We will also be trying to engage Russia productively at other G8 discussions, in the context of the NATO-Russia Council, as well as in the Organization for Security and Cooperation in Europe, and at the Conference on Disarmament. On all of these fronts, collaboration will be greatly helped by the deep respect for multilateralism and international law that Canada and Russia share.

And on other issues of global concern, Canada and Russia are also working together: for example, through CIDA we are helping Russia face its growing AIDS crisis; and we are tackling environmental issues through the Arctic Council and through a Russia-Canada joint working group on climate change. In the face of international terrorism and the terrible hostage-taking at the Moscow theatre by Chechen rebels last fall, Canada has emphasized to Russia the importance of responding to national security threats while respecting human rights. I raised these concerns with Foreign Minister Ivanov while in Moscow, particularly in respect of the internally displaced people who are at risk. It's a tribute to the maturity of our relationship that we are able to share our concerns about highly sensitive issues such as these in a spirit of mutual respect."

Mention of these large global issues brings me finally to the topic of Canada's foreign policy consultations. In January, I launched these consultations in order to update our foreign policy in face of changes and challenges that have arisen over the past decade, since our last major review. I'm asking Canadians to look at a discussion paper we've released, called *A Dialogue on Foreign Policy*, and to give me their views on a list of twelve questions. Many of these questions, in fact, bear closely on the sorts of issues I've touched on today: what kind of security arrangements we'll need in view of new types of threats, and how we can work bilaterally and multilaterally with Russia and other nations to meet these threats; what kind of global measures we can take to fight disease, environmental degradation, and the spread of weapons of mass destruction; how Canada can best promote our prosperity by forging new economic relationships; and how we can better promote Canadian values and culture in Russia and elsewhere.

In view of your interest and expertise in foreign affairs – and in a country as important as Russia – I hope that all of you will take the time to contribute to this consultation process before it wraps up on May 1. You can download the Dialogue paper and give your answers on-line, if you wish, by going to our Web site, which has excellent interactive features and information resources. The Web site address is: http://www.foreign-policy-dialogue.ca/. The views of engaged Canadians such as yourselves will be crucial to our efforts at updating Canada's foreign policy for the years to come.

So in conclusion, I thank you for having invited me here today to speak on such an important topic. The Russia of today would have been unimaginable fifteen or twenty years ago, and Canada and the world certainly benefit from the developments that have taken place in Russia over the past decade. We look forward to strengthening the ties between our countries in the years to come. And of course a great asset in that effort will be a pool of informed Canadians who will have the knowledge to facilitate political, economic and cultural exchanges. So I congratulate the student organizers of this conference for choosing to focus on these issues today, and on behalf of the Government of Canada I welcome the contributions that your studies, as well of those of the experts here today, will make to the well-being of both Canada and Russia in the years to come.

Canada-Russia Relations: A Russian View
His Excellency Vitaly Churkin, Ambassador of the Russian
Federation to Canada

Yesterday, over dinner I was told many interesting things about Glendon College. One of them is that you happen to be a perfectly bilingual College, but today I want to come up with a major initiative: I heard more Russian spoken this morning than maybe the two other languages, English or French, so the initiative is that maybe starting from today we could call it a perfectly trilingual College. In fact I am tempted to deliver my remarks in Russian. I am sure that most of those present would understand me without any problem and much of the content is going to be reflected by Mr. Graham's speech as well.

If there is a need for further proof of the excellent state of relations between Russia and Canada, this will definitely be the participation of Minister Graham in today's discussion. We are certainly privileged to be in his company today. I would also like to note that in my history book Ms McDougall does play a very special role as I vividly remember her welcoming President Yelstin during his first visit to Canada in February of 1992 when Ms McDougall was heading Canadian diplomacy, so in a certain way she was part of the creation of new relations between our countries. In fact, President Yeltsin liked the trip so much that just five months later in July 1992, he returned for a big state visit, which is a very rare occurrence in diplomatic practice. On that occasion a major treaty was signed between Canada and Russia, which marked a new beginning in a new relationship between Russia as a democratic country and Canada as an old friend. I am also glad to appear today on the same panel with Anne Leahy. She was the one who, as Canadian Ambassador to Moscow, gave me a farewell lunch and best wishes on my trip to Canada. Thank you very much, Anne, I have been just fine! So your wishes have not been wasted on me!

Something surprised me just months after I arrived in Canada as Ambassador in the fall of 1998. We all know there are quite a few things in common between our two countries: the climate, the large territories, the natural resources, etc. But it came as a surprise to me that our countries, despite their different political backgrounds and the fact that they are located on different continents, they see the world in many respects in the same way. There are fundamental principles, which Canada and modern democratic Russia share as they look at the world, and that is what makes our cooperation in the international arena so important and productive.

We share a respect for international law and an understanding of the importance of upholding this international order. We also share an understanding of the importance of the United Nations in this world. We share an understanding of the importance of arms control demonstrated in our attempts to preserve and enhance the regime, which was created in order to produce a more peaceful and secure world.

Just to give you a few examples of our shared principles, first of all, Russia and Canada are at this point very active diplomatic partners in trying to work out an international agreement, which would prevent the militarization of outer space. Our two countries are also active partners in a number of international forums. The G8 summit in Kananaskis, which was presided over by Prime Minister Jean Chrétien; resulted in very important decisions as far as Russia is concerned. One is that Russia is becoming a full member of the G8 and is going to hold the presidency in 2006, including the summit and other G8 meetings. Secondly, a major program was adopted for global partnership in the prevention of proliferation of weapons and materials of mass destruction. The importance of this program for Russia is that, among other things, we have inherited from the Soviet Union a lage stockpile of completely unnecessary weapons of mass destruction – mostly chemical weapons and also de-commissioned nuclear submarines – stationed in the northern and far eastern seas, threatening to pollute the environment. So, a major international effort has been launched, which will begin to deal with that legacy. Moreover, Russia and Canada are important members of the anti-terrorist coalition, and along with dealing with this issue internationally, we have established a number of bilateral channels between our countries, where our experts share information and help chart the course of our joined struggle against this curse of the 21st century.

On the economic front, things are not as cheerful as we would like them to be. Russian-Canadian trade ranges at US $100 million dollars, which is, of course, a negligible sum, compared to the potential of our countries. Investment levels are not impressive either. The problem, I think, as we analyze our nations is that there is not one single major project, which would symbolically represent our economic relationship.

Nonetheless, many important things are happening in our economic relations. SLCC, a Montreal-based company, is involved in as many as a dozen projects in Russia, and I think some of them are very promising. Bombardier is present in Russia both with skidoos and in the railroad renovation industry. There are some disappointments; we are not always off to a very good start. For example, it is logical for Canadian mining, oil, and gas companies to be heavily involved in Russia, and they did start to create a presence in the early 90's, but the experience was not very successful. Sometimes mistakes were made on their behalf; sometimes they encountered competition; and sometimes numerous complaints were made about (and this is a serious complaint, which we recognize) our legal system. The Russian government considers the reform of the legal system a major priority and as rule of law is consolidated in Russia, foreign companies will have better conditions to invest.

I must tell you frankly that Russians have similar problems with Canada, so please do not think of it as unilateral grievance, which Canadian businessmen have in Russia. We are very disappointed that our exports of steel into Canada have dwindled to zero. It used to be Russia's major export article totalling US $200 million dollars annually, but these exports have been hit by anti-dumping moves, some of which were not always fair. We have some other problems which could have been solved more rapidly to the benefit of our economic relations. However, this is what the embassy, the diplomats, and the governments are for. Our job includes trying to help businesses deal with such issues.

On the governmental side, of course, we are trying to facilitate Russian-Canadian economic relations, and periodic meetings are held to discuss these matters. The major highlight of our business relationship was, of course, the visit by Prime Minister Chrétien to Russia in February 2002, which resulted in the signing of dozens of contracts, not only in economic, but also in academic and cultural fields. Most recently, the Russian and Canadian Chambers of Commerce signed their first agreement, which we hope will make contacts and cooperation between business people easier and more productive.

There are plenty of other areas of very important cooperation. Cultural cooperation is flourishing. The Hermitage is having an exhibition in Montreal. There was a Hermitage exhibition in Toronto before, and there will be another one in Toronto later. I am also proud of the fact that the Russian Consulate General has opened in Toronto. Believe it or not, Russia did not have any diplomatic presence at all in Toronto, which has a very special significance because not only it is a financial and economic centre, but also the seat of a large and, I must say with gratitude, very friendly Russian community.

As a sign of increasingly close cooperation between Russia and Canada, the past two years have seen most members of the two governments get in touch and get to know each other. Minister Graham made a very important visit to Russia last November and President Putin was here on a state visit two years ago. The Russian Prime Minister Kasyanov visited Canada. Let us hope that the positive trends in Russian-Canadian relations will develop even more vigorously in the coming years.

Russia in Search of a Place in a Changing World
Doctor Nikolai Zlobin, Centre for Defense Information

Nearly everything in Russia has changed over the past twelve years. The Soviet Union was a country where changes, if they occurred at all, tended to proceed at a glacial pace. But after 1991, visitors were shocked by how different things looked. 'Each visit is like seeing a whole new country', was the typical reaction. But with time, it became increasingly clear that rapid change does not indicate deep-rooted change. Behind the new façade, real life was changing much more slowly and hesitantly than it first seemed. The running joke was that 'Russia is a country in which everything changes and everything remains the same'. Certain facets of Russian life and political culture lagged behind others, and a socio-political disequilibrium increased in intensity, exposing contradictions between areas of life and government where changes were obvious, and those where everything stayed nearly the same. The latter ones, moreover, included such important areas of government as agriculture, the banking system, military reform and foreign policy.

After 1991, Russian foreign policy, despite all the changes in rhetoric, is not characterized by any new fundamental approaches or systemic conceptualizations. In many ways, it is still based on perceptions of the world that had formed in the years of the Cold War.[1] As K. Gadzhiev writes, "Russia cannot help but be a great power for the simple reason that it holds a special place in the geopolitical structure of the world".[2] To this day, the major focus of activity for the country's foreign policy structures is national security, in the narrow sense of the word. It is the yardstick by which Russian diplomats and politicians measure the modern world. "For Russia", continues Gadzhiev, "the issue is about security in all its aspects and measurements: global, regional, national, as well as political, economic, social, ecological, informational...The major strategic task for Russia's foreign policy organs is to ensure a stable and safe environment".[3]

Such an approach, more fit for the Defense Ministry, sets Moscow apart from the European powers, whose foreign policy has long been based on other principles and priorities, primarily social, economic, and humanitarian ones.[4] But after September 11, national security, homeland defense, and the protection of national interests became the main foreign policy agenda of the US as well. Russia, it seemed, had gained the most powerful of potential allies.

When Russian President Putin spoke of full and unqualified support for the US, this was viewed as a strategic choice, made by the Russian leadership, and suited the interests of both countries, as well as 'a revolution in Russian foreign policy'. Russia took the American tragedy as its own; thousands of people bearing flowers surrounded the US embassy in Moscow. The talk around town was that 'America would now understand Russia better; it will be much easier for us to find a common language'. On the same day, NATO invoked Paragraph 6 of is charter, regarding the collective response of NATO members to an attack on a single member. And thus, in one day, Russia found itself in the company of the most powerful countries in the world, united by a common vision of global problems and threats. But in just a few months, Russian-American relations went into a severe decline. Europe began to actively push Russia away, and Russia herself took a position that facilitated the European split, a result which clearly contradicted Russia's security interests. Neither Europe nor the US can be held blameless for the foreign policy mistakes and miscalculations of the past two years, but in this article, I will concentrate on Moscow's foreign policy positions.

'The strategic choice of 9/11' has not, so far, turned out to be strategic. For the past two years, the Kremlin has failed to put into practice Russia's 'strategic choice', as it has also neglected to convince Russian society and political elites of its rationale. In truth, the Kremlin has not taken any visible steps toward realizing that choice. If such a revolution did take place, it was contained within the presidential cabinet. It seems after all that "Russian geopolitics is not endowed with the necessary economic and organizational resources".[5]

Russia in the System of International Relations

The end of the Cold War invalidated a system of international relations and a political philosophy that had existed over the past half century. But within that system, Russia was able to play a leading role, acting as a countervailing force to the US.[6] The Cold War acclimated us to predictability, stability, and a primitive foreign policy. It prevented the outbreak of a hot war – that has been its historic merit. America required more than ten years after the collapse of the USSR to define new principles of national security and to begin to realize the degree of her own responsibility in the world. Europe has been unable to formulate its foreign policy, and lives in a self-constructed reality. It's difficult to imagine how many years it will take for Russia to find its place in this new world.

Nearly all concepts in international relations demand revision. Until recently, the necessary criteria for an international alliance was the unity of social values, for instance: democracy, free markets, or socialism. Now, alliances are built around practical concerns, geopolitical opportunities, and common geopolitical goals. These conditions present difficulties for Russia. First, internal weaknesses make Russia a less appealing partner. Second, countries that have traditionally been a part of the Russian sphere of influence or sought a close relationship with her – Uzbekistan, Georgia, the Baltic states, Poland, and Bulgaria – have expressed increasing interest in a partnership with the US and NATO. Under these conditions, there are limited places Moscow can look to form independent blocs – parts of Central Asia, Belorussia, and Armenia.

The fundamentals of international alliances have shifted. They now have a much more ephemeral character, since none of the partners wants to make long-term promises and live with the consequences; the situation is changing so fast that the national elites are unable to comprehend the true meaning of events as they occur. The response of Russia's foreign policy elites toward American actions in Iraq are a typical example. Alliances are formed to solve concrete, limited problems, after which countries can feel free to go their own ways. Who knows, next time they may meet as enemies. Yet this is unacceptable to Russia, who wants a much more formalized mode of relations, especially with the US. The agreement to reduce nuclear weapons, which has little meaning in practice, was concluded in May of 2002 at Moscow's insistence. The US offered an informal agreement. Moscow insists on a formal rejection of the Jackson-Vanick Amendment and the formalization of all agreements with the European Union.

The concepts of war, security, and military strength have all changed, which creates new threats for Russia – a country that has lost her military superiority and the opportunity to independently ensure her security. Wars are now conducted, as a rule, without much contact between the forces. The focus is not on a surprise attack on the enemy, but upon its forces of communication. The goal is not military victory, but a change of the regime or its policies. There is nothing unique about this: regime changes took place in Russia, in the countries of Eastern Europe and the former USSR of the 1990s.

Moscow and Washington have fundamental disagreements on the topic of which countries present the greatest threat to the world. Moscow thinks that these countries include Georgia, Saudi Arabia, or Pakistan, whose rockets can reach its territory, while Iraq did not present any direct threat. But the Russian army is unable to conduct a modern war, and any traditional war in which it participates would not lead to stability in dangerous regions. This adds to Moscow's existing economic and political weakness. That is why its role in making these kind of decisions is today quite minimal.

Russia and International Organizations

The Second World War demolished practically all international organizations that appeared in the first half of the century, and replaced them with new ones. The UN was born to replace the League of Nations, which proved ineffective in times of conflict, and to guarantee that no one from the Allied coalition would conclude a separate peace with the Axis powers. In 1945, the UN Security Council included five victorious nations, and its composition at the time seemed logical and fair.

But given the current situation, it is hard to justify the international importance of a country based on the outcome of World War II. The second and third largest economies in the world – Japan and Germany – play a much more important role in global governance than, say, Russia, but are nevertheless excluded from the Security Council. Also excluded is India, with almost a billion people, and Indonesia, the fifth most populous country in the world. Globalization, the formation of the European Union, the technological revolution, and nuclear proliferation speeded up the breakdown of the post-war hierarchies to an even greater extent. In many world capitals, today's UN appears illogical and unjust. Long before the collapse of the USSR, the UN had become a bureaucratic structure that concerned itself not with political issues but with global welfare, education, and health. The enormous changes in the world system over the past 15 years have occurred without any UN involvement.

The UN's strength is to a large extent based on the lack of competition and on long-standing ties with the national elites of many countries who use the UN to make cosmetic improvements to their international images, something they cannot accomplish with changes in policy. The recent debates over the war in Iraq demonstrated this perfectly. After the Kremlin had become an insignificant political player, it became acutely obvious that the UN was unable to solve the major political problems of modernity, the nature of which had been drastically altered. The UN was unable to deal with Chechnya, international terrorism, genocide in Serbia and Ethiopia as well as the Middle East, Afghanistan, nuclear proliferation, the drug trade, etc.

What is needed is either a truly radical reform of the UN, or its replacement by a fundamentally new international organization that can adequately respond to the changing global order. Moscow, however, takes a very cautious view on this position, championing the 'leading role of the UN' while skirting the issue of its ineffectiveness.[7] The fight against international terrorism could become the beginning of the collapse of the UN in its present form, which corresponds to the historical logic as well as to the desires of the US administration. Any UN reforms would inevitably diminish Moscow's status even more, a result that Moscow would oppose to the bitter end, since the Security Council is Moscow's last bastion to exert influence in the international pantheon. For Russia to attain such a high level of importance is simply impossible in the foreseeable future. That is precisely why Putin states that any UN reforms must proceed "not only within a UN framework, but also with the use of procedures, implicit in the norms of international law as recognized by the UN".[8] In other words, with Russia's decisive participation.

Upon coming to power, Putin proclaimed, "Russia should build its foreign policy on the basis of a clear delineation of national priorities, pragmatism, and economic effectiveness".[9] After WWII, the USSR took an extremely calculated and active position, thereby ensuring for itself all the influential positions in all the major international structures. This allowed the USSR to play a key role in the world during the second half of the 20th century. Today, the scenario is partially replaying itself. Russia, of course, doesn't have the advantages that the USSR held at the time. And yet before Iraq, it was in the same camp as the US. The alliance with Washington is crucial for Moscow in many respects. The

EU plan for accepting 12 new members from Eastern and Southern Europe will be the last expansion of that organization for the near future. The same can be said for NATO. Europeans will not be concerning themselves with Russia's place in Europe for at least the next half-century.

But the Russian position on Iraq was also an obvious deviation from Putin's proclaimed pragmatism. By taking a stand against the American actions, Moscow intensified the crisis within the Security Council. If the US and, following them, England, exit the UN or simply refuse to take a part in its activities, then Russia will be the biggest loser. In attempting to prevent war, Russian succeeded in marshaling the march towards it, unwittingly facilitating the schism in the UN and weakening the EU's position, which runs contrary to Russia's own interests. Her position exacerbated the contradictions within NATO, and led to an increased role of NATO's East European members, which complicates the execution of Russian foreign policy's agenda toward Europe. Moscow's actions helped create a deep and perhaps intractable crisis in the Security Council.

At one time, 'the Big Seven' was an attempt to find a new method of coordinating Western interests outside of UN structures. But with the end of the Cold War, the political importance of these countries rapidly diminished, and their agenda underwent some fundamental changes. Paradoxically, with the inclusion of Russia as a permanent participant in 2001, as well as the invitation to China to attend its meetings, the 'Big Eight' now has another chance to become a place for serious international discussion on the most important issues of the day. Russia, which now holds one of the leading positions in this group, will undoubtedly try to not only submit its agenda and actively participate in the meetings, but also transform these meetings into a vehicle for addressing global problems important to Russia.

We could suppose that, in attempting to compensate for the depth of its presence on the global scene, Russia will strive toward quantity over quality, and express an interest in participating in various international organizations and structures that it may have once ignored. Significant foreign policy efforts will be directed toward that goal.

Russia and the Bush Doctrine

Traditionally, politics are built on agreements and relations among sovereign states. In the past twenty-five years, globalizing forces in economics have taken the economy beyond the control of individual states. Multinational corporations easily broke down the barriers of traditional financial and labour markets. Russia found itself completely removed from this process. The euro now supplements the dollar as a transnational currency. Technological developments in the sphere of communications and the proliferation of the Internet have threatened the existence of national media structures, and with that, the possibility of sovereign governments to control their country's media, and consequently, the national ideology. The freedom of movement of goods, people, money and information have led to the state's loss of its traditional spheres of control. For the leadership of a weakened Russia, this has created a host of new problems.

Numerous political players have appeared on the international scene who are not formalized in the form of states, and not subject to any sovereign government. One example of such structures is al-Qaida, or the terrorist organizations in Chechnya. They cannot sign treaties or exchange ambassadors; they cannot be penalized with sanctions or embargoes. Some governments offer them assistance, but it's nearly impossible to catch someone red-handed. Certainly, they cannot be defeated via traditional methods at least in part because they do not fall under the jurisdiction of international law, which only applies to sovereign states. The Geneva Conventions, for instance, do not mention terrorists at all. Russia's methods for restoring order in Chechnya cause a storm of indignation in the West.

But the world society does not have the means to combat these structures. The old doctrine of containment, and the system of international law that formalized it, turned out to be unfit for the task, since it was based on the containment of one state by another, and functioned through the accumulation of political influence and military power by various states. But terrorist acts in the US showed that neither an enormous military budget, nor an ultra-modern and technologically enhanced army, nor a computerized police system, is able to protect its people from an attack. The most developed state, whose military budget exceeds the military budget of the next 12 countries put together, could not perform its basic function – the provision of security for its citizens. America was the best-equipped country to protect itself from any other state, but the attack did not come from a state-based entity. Russia has also encountered this problem, both in its counter-terrorist measures and in Chechnya.

The inevitability of a stand-off between sovereign states and transnational non-governmental entities who reject the very idea of national sovereignty has become a common problem. One can demand a cessation of terrorist actions from the Chechen leadership, but it is not clear whether they control their own territory. Vladimir Putin is right, in his own way, for refusing to negotiate with Aslan Maskhadov, who is to a great degree a 'virtual' leader. But, on the other hand, Putin himself does not control all the structures operating within Russia.

'Limited sovereignty' is becoming the new reality of a globalized world. If previously, the emergency of a new threat could be counteracted by strengthening border defence and bringing the army to an alert state, then today such actions are meaningless. Hence the notion of a pre-emptive strike as a way of ensuring national security.

It would be incorrect to say that this idea refutes the doctrine of containment, or that it is something entirely new. Preventive actions and limited sovereignty were for a long time a part of the Brezhnev Doctrine, and were invoked to justify actions by the Soviet Union in socialist countries, like Hungary in 1956 and Czechoslovakia in 1968. But before the main focus was on a counter-strike. The aggressor knew that in case of an attack, he could expect a response. Today, if he refuses to disarm despite the demand of the international community, he can expect a pre-emptive strike. Of course, this concept is highly debatable and dangerous, and fraught with unpredictable consequences. But it is not a manifestation of an imperial mindset but rather an admission that after the Cold War, the containment doctrine is no longer able to prevent conflict and, moreover, to effectively disarm the developed countries in the face of a new threat. This is an admission of the fact that modern states are continuing to lose their traditional functions, and are no longer able to ensure either their own or their allies' safety, and that their borders and defence systems are becoming less reliable. To prevent the doctrine of pre-emptive strike from becoming the dominant mode of the global order, a new conceptualization must be proffered. This new approach must practically replace the doctrine of containment, which has passed into history, but not represent an effort to return the US to the old legal framework, as some experts suggest.[10]

For many reasons, this question is more relevant for Russia than for many other parts of the world. That is why any criticism that Russia puts forth of the pre-emptive strike doctrine focuses not on the idea itself, but on the question of methods, and the circumstances under which such a decision can be made. In Moscow's opinion, the UN should be the decision-making body, and should, as Evgeny Primakov wrote, "be maintained as the only organization that sanctions the use of force."[11] But it could also be assumed that Moscow will accept the basic elements of the Bush Doctrine as the major instrument of foreign policy in the world today, as long as it allows Russia a prominent voice in the decision-making process, either on a bilateral level or within the G-8 framework.

Russia and International Terrorism

Russia and the US diverge in their understanding of the nature of international terrorism. Moscow will have to make its choice in the near future. Until Iraq, the Russian position was close to the European one, but the Euro-Russian union did not develop after the end of the military operations in Iraq by the US and UK troops.[12]

Russian leadership treats international terrorists mostly as a new type of criminal, or criminal elements united into certain structures. Chechen fighters or al-Qaeda are seen as a kind of modern mafia, Islamic rather than Sicilian, but with other connotations intact. Moscow believes that this threat should be combated by strengthening the police, laws, and the passport's regimes, as well as increasing control over the territory through periodic 'clean-outs', or sweeps. Chechen fighters are depicted as criminals who benefit by exploiting the Chechen people's desire for independence.

Washington, on the other hand, views modern international terrorism as a socio-political phenomenon, an international movement that is political and ideological, rather than criminal, in nature. They see a movement that vies neither for economic gain nor for concessions from particular governments, but for the destruction of the very fundamentals of our civilization, the replacement of one system of basic values for another. They must be opposed, therefore, not as basic criminals, but as sworn foes, using all the military force available. A particular threat is the potential for terrorists to come to power, as occurred in Afghanistan. Russia, incidentally, supported the elimination of the Taliban in Afghanistan from the very beginning, viewing it as a real threat to its national security, albeit for different reasons. The alliance of terrorists and governments greatly enhances terrorism's destructive capabilities, complicates any struggle against it, and facilitates terrorists' access to weapons of mass destruction. Terrorist Islamic groups that possess such weapons pose the greatest threat to global security now.

The US views contemporary Islamist extremism and terrorism through the same lens as communism and fascism – a perspective, which Russia, with her proximity to Islamic territories and a large Muslim population, cannot afford to adopt. Yet Moscow cannot forget that al-Qaeda considers (and has used) the old continent not as an object for attack, but as a base of preparations for new assaults, potentially on Russia as well. The Russian approach, aimed at fighting particular groups in response to particular acts, is at odds with the White House strategy of unfolding a wide-scale war against Islamic extremism and terrorism.

Russia's strategy of fighting international terrorism is only now taking shape. As G. Pavlovsky notes, "none of the existing structures of international security – including NATO, the EU, CIS, OSCE, the Collective Security Agreement – can fully guarantee Russia a place in the world that would place it at ease, from a strategic viewpoint."[13] Iskander Khisamov suggests that Russia cannot "fit into any of the existing global alliances".[14] Islamist extremism is bent on revenge of historic proportions, attempting to recapture what it lost under the last few centuries of Western domination. Only naïvete would suggest the violence will stop at the Russian border because of the Kremlin's threat to veto the Security Council resolution on Iraq. Still more naïve is the supposition that Europe will suddenly concern itself with the problems of Russian security, when it is already in no hurry to assist the US.

Russia and the US after Iraq

The US-Russian summit held in St. Petersburg in June 2003 was a troubling symptom of the lack of fundamentals in Russian-American relations. It once again revealed a tendency to ignore deep-seated problems and serious mutual disagreements, which have brought today's strategic partnership to the verge of bankruptcy.

Relations between the two countries are at their lowest point in the past ten years. "Russia and the US no longer compete for spheres of influence",[15] noted Colin Powell. And yet the differences over Iraq have forced us to see what we had previously ignored. There are sharp, fundamental, perhaps even insoluble differences between Russia and the US – in their approach to building a new world order and a system of global security, in their understanding of contemporary threats and how they must be met, and in their attitude toward international law. Russia has been moved to the bottom of Washington's list of countries that the American establishment considers key potential partners. The Russian foreign policy establishment, for its part, has had to abandon the long-cherished myth that America is in vital need of an alliance with Russia and would be unable to take decisive action anywhere in the world without it. 'The trustworthy partnership', of which Putin spoke in July of 2002, has not materialized.[16] The conflict over Iraq ended an entire era of productive relations. After a period of searching for a strategic partnership, we have entered a period of possible cooperation on a number of issues where the two countries' interests coincide. It's not a secret that practically all these common interests revolve around security and energy, but this does not yet guarantee their success.[17]

Despite the sustained criticism of the Bush Administration's handling of foreign policy, we must face the facts: Russia's stance on Iraq resulted in a loss it could ill afford. Moscow's position was removed from simple pragmatism; it did not correspond to the country's economic or national interests. It was, therefore, in direct contradiction to Russia's proclaimed foreign policy principles. This cannot be blamed simply on a unilateral approach to bilateral relations, which the US has indeed sometimes demonstrated, from steel protectionism to Jackson-Vanick, to forcing Russia out of Afghanistan, for example.

The situation with Iraq demonstrated that Russia not only lacks an understanding of today's global developments, but does not even have a strategically focused foreign policy. The president is not the only one to blame for this. Russia has neither the infrastructure nor the intellectual potential to prepare an adequate analysis of global events, provide realistic forecasts, or develop an optimal behaviour model for the country on the international arena. The individuals and institutions assigned to these tasks were unable to handle them. There is absolutely no evidence that Putin is powerful enough to persist in his wishes alone. Moscow demonstrated an unacceptable amount of improvisation, and as is well known, an unpredictable friend is worse than a predictable foe. Taking into account Russia's nuclear status, an improvisational foreign policy is more than a sovereign policy, but also one that could detrimentally affect other global developments.

Since the end of the Cold War, I protested against the thesis of 'the necessity for improving Russian-American relations', trying to show that one cannot improve something that was created for different political and international realities.[18] We should not try to improve relations that are not, by definition, improvable, but form new bilateral relations on a fundamentally different conceptual basis, one that has yet to take shape. One can improve a steam engine up to a certain point, but after that, the engine requires a qualitative jump to the next power source. Both sides spent more than a decade 'improving the steam engine', and yet today have no coherent policy toward each other to show for their efforts.

The conflict over Iraq became the conceptual bankrupting of the model of Russian-American relations that we have pursued over the past decade. And when there is no overarching conception for relations, when there are no fundamentals, then any disagreements – whether over Iraq or poultry – expand to an enormous size, since we have no fulcrum with which to position ourselves in search of a solution. We can already see that the nearing conflict over Iran[19] has the potential to become much more serious.[20]

George Bush sympathizes with Putin outside the context of bilateral relations; his affinity for the Russian president transcends the political relations of the two countries. Clinton was also friends with Yeltsin, as he believed Yeltsin would be able to bring democracy to Russia. Bush's attitude toward Putin is based on personal factors and does not rely on an ongoing evaluation of political processes in Russia. Bush is the most pro-Russian US president in modern history, and in the absence of cultural or political unity or significant economic cooperation between these two countries, mutual trust of the presidents is vital capital indeed. But as important as the Bush-Putin friendship is, it is not what Russia needs right now. It needs not only a well thought-out, solid foreign policy and a fresh elite that can develop one, but also a properly institutionalized structure for its effective implementation. Otherwise, when Moscow makes a strategic decision, sometime in the future, its implementation ones again will not extend beyond the president's office.

Russia's Choices

Of course, there are a number of very important directions in Russian foreign policy that I have yet to touch upon. Relations with China or Europe[21], for instance are critically important, and require a separate discussion. Russia's positions on Iran or North Korea are in a state of change and their outcomes may have profound consequences. Russia has many interests around the world. As D. Trenin writes, Russia can be described as a country that's "Euro-Pacific, open to the outside world and striving for 'special relations' with the global leader – the US. In the West, the EU has become the major regional partner, and in the East, Japan may and should become such a partner as well".[22] But all these strains in the Russian national interest are united by one factor – they are all secondary, derivative of the issues I have already mentioned here. Russia must first define the fundamental questions of the new world order, and decide what place Russia wants (and can realistically secure) in the new century, and how it can ensure her own unity, security, and well-being.

Russia's military weakness is a new factor, and it needs to be rectified. Can Europe compensate for it? G. Pavlovsky notes that Russia has more unregulated issues with Europe than with the US.[23] Europe's military weakness is not a new phenomena – it was obvious immediately after the Second World War. But until recently, this weakness was camouflaged by the tremendous military support that Europe was offered by the US. For Russia, it is important that transatlantic tensions do not undermine international security, since it is situated much closer to the world's powder keg than either Europeans or Americans. Recently, the Chairman on the Council on Foreign and Defence Policy S. Karaganov concluded that Moscow should "revise its policy toward Europe, since it is based on an unrealistic conception of trends in the Old World".[24]

A serious, non-ideological discussion on foreign policy questions is desperately lacking in Russia today.[25] Debates take place within a now-traditional framework of criticizing Washington's hegemony. Putin criticizes the Anglo-American occupation of Iraq, but does not provide evidence that a (say) Euro-Russian occupation would be more successful. Moscow is against a unipolar world because it functions without Russia. But there is no evidence that a multipolar world would provide Russia with more security than a unipolar one. Multipolarity is less stable and predictable, and it will not necessarily lead to a greater global role for Russia, which can no longer be an independent power center. But if Russia and the US can agree on a new relationship paradigm, then Russia has a much greater chance of gaining from a unipolar world without having to engage in certain, undesirable compromises.

Only recently, it seemed that the Russian elite was on the brink of an intellectual breakthrough, but instead, Moscow intellectuals engaged themselves in a discourse on how, if Russia is to ally with America, Russia should be the head while America should be the fist and the bankbook. The talk of empire has emerged once again. A. Dugin assures that Russia is "an empire, by geopolitical logic, that this time around should surpass USSR, the previous variant, both strategically and territorially. The new empire, therefore, should be Eurasian, continental, and global in perspective".[26] S. Karaganov thinks that the main weakness of Russia's foreign policy is the weakness of the Russian economy.[27] Others speak of Russia taking a middle stance between Europe, Asia, and the US, becoming politically equidistant to the great world powers. Russia today, says V. Lukin, "returns to Europe with the accoutrements of totally new relations with the US. This gives Russia an historic chance to occupy the niche of a 'transatlantic integrator' – a country that exists in the political space between two analytic opposites, taking upon itself the mission of eliminating diplomatic lacunae, attempting to become the catalyst and the initiator of trilateral political actions".[28] Lukin is convinced that no one else can claim such a role. S. Rogov says that

Russia can only be rescued by a "middleman position on the geopolitical map of Eurasia".[29] It is unclear why the powers need such a middleman – and if they do need one, why would they turn to Moscow, which is notorious for being unable to reach compromises in foreign relations?

After the war in Iraq, Russia faces the difficult task of overcoming the consequences of its only serious mistake in foreign policy over the past ten years. It needs clear positions on the theories of building global structures, theories that are incubating now in the White House. At the same time, the Kremlin cannot become a hostage of the political struggle among the various factions in the White House administration.[30] The issue here is Russia's place in the new world order, in the new system of global security that will replace the one that had existed for the last fifty years. The major question is whether Russia – either in a close alliance with the US or without one – can ensure an optimally advantageous position in the world and safeguard the strategic security of her interests. A clear answer has yet to be articulated.

Notes

[1] Herman Pirchner, "With or Against the West: Russia's Debate Continue; *Demokratizatsiya*, 11.1 (2003): 51-54.

[2] K. Gadzhiev, "Ot bipolarnosti k novoy konfiguratsii geopolitichskikh sil" in *Vneshnyaya politika I bezopasnost sovremennoy Rossii*, 1, Moscow, Mosckovskiy Obschestvenny Nauchnyi Fond, (1999): 69.

[3] Ibid, 70.

[4] *Rossiya i osnovniye institute bezopasnosti v Evrope: vstupaya v XX vek*; Moskva, Fond Karnegi za mezhdunarodniy mir, 2000.

[5] *Geopolticheskoye polozheniye Rossii: predstavleniya i realnost*; ed, V. Kolosov, Moskva, Art-Kourier, 2000: 336.

[6] *Rossia is SShA posle kholodnoy voyni*, ed, V. Kremenyuk; Moskva, Nauka, 1999.

[7] Igor Ivanov, *Mezhdunarodnaya bezopasnost v epokhy globalizatsii*, in "Rossiya v Globalnoy Politike", 1, January-March 2003, 47.

[8] Vladimir Putin, "Modernizatsiya OON dolzhna prokhodit tolko v ramkakh samoy OON," RTR-Vesti, 2003, April 12, <www.vesti.ru/news.html?pid=30393>.

[9] Full text of the address by Vladimir Putin to the Federal Council, April 3 2002, <www.vremya.ru/cgi-bin/print/2002/59/events/1590.html>

[10] Sergey Rogov, "Igra bez Pravil", *Moskovsky Komsomolets*, April 11, 2003.

[11] Evgeny Primakov, "Mezhdunardoniye otnosheniya nakanune XX veka: problemy, perspektivy" In *Mezhdunaronaya Zhizn,* 1996, 10, 12.

[12] Andrei Reut, "Putin, Schroeder i Shirak pozhalovalis drug drugu na Busha i Blera" in *Gazeta,* April 14, 2003.

[13] Gleb Pavlovsky, "Novaya bipolyarnaya simmetriya – novoye mirovoye mesto Rossii" in *Natsionalnaya laboratoriya vneshney politiki*, July 16, 2002; <www.nlvp/ru/print/24/html>.

[14] Iskander Khisamov, "Vybor Kontserta" in *Ekspert*, 9, March 10, 2003.

[15] Colin Powell, "Rossiya i SShA ne boroyutsia za sfery vliyaniya" in *Nezavisimaya Gazeta*, October 16, 2002.

[16] Address of the President of the Russian Federation V.V. Putin in the expanded hearing with the ambassadors of the Russian Federation in the Russian Foreign Ministry. July 12, 2002; Moscow, 2002, 4.

[17] See Maksim Blunt, "Vtoroy Front" in *Ezhenedelnyi Zhurnal*, 18, Sep. 20, 2002.

[18] Nikolai Zlobin, "The United States: Russia and New Challenges" *Demokratizatsiya*, 11.1, (2003): 44-54.

[19] In 2002 the Russian government approved a long-term partnership program with Iran, according to which over the next ten years, six more nuclear reactors besides the Busher one will be built, for a total cost of over ten billion dollars. See, for example, www.gazeta.ru/2002/08/01/mezdurossiej.shtml.

[20] See Vladimir Rudakov, "Teheran-03" in *Ekspert*, #21, June 9, 2003, 28-29.

[21] This is especially complicated by the fact that according to demographers, by 2010 the Chinese may become the second largest ethnic group in Russia, after Russians, reaching 8-10 million in number. See Andrei Vaganov, "Da! Aziati mi..." in *Nezavisimaya Gazeta*, August 6, 2002.

[22] Dmitry Trenin, "Evro-Tikhookeanskaya Derzhava" in *Rossiya v Globalnoy Politike*, 1, Jan-March 2003, 34.

[23] Pavlovsky (2002) [see endnote 14]

[24] Sergey Karaganov, "U Rossii est unikalniy vneshnepoliticheskii resurs" in *Nezavisimaya Gazeta,* May 12, 2003.

[25] Aleksei Kiva, "SShA rvutsiya k mirovomu gospodstvu" in *Nezavisimaya Gazeta,* Jan. 28, 2003; Lyuba Shariy, "Drakan posle Iraka. SShA mogut sdelat stavky na razval Rossii" in *Moskovskiy Komsomolets,* April 11, 2003; Aleksander Golts, "Gordiev Uzel: glavnym rezultatom antiteroristicheskoy operatsii stalo ustanovleniye bezuslovnoy gegemonii SShA" in *Ezhenedelny Zhurnal,* 35, (2002):11-16.

[26] Aleksander Dugin, *Osnovy geopolitiki. Geopolticheskoy buduscheye Rossii;* Moskva, Arktogeya, (1997): 213.

[27] *Sovremennaya rossiskaya politika,* edited by V.Nikonov; Moskva, Olma-Press, (2003): 186.

[28] Vladimir Lukin, "Rossiyskiy most cherez Atlantiku" in *Rossiya v Globalnoy POlitike,* 1, Nov. – Dec (2002): 103.

[29] Sergeu Rogov, "Kontury novoy rossiiskoy strategii" in *Nezavisimaya Gazeta – Stsenarii,* 3, March 2003.

[30] See Colin Powell, "Rossia sama dolzhna reshit, chto ey delat dlia samozaschiti" in *Izvestiya,* October 23, 2002.

Continuity and Change in Russian Foreign Policy
Professor Sergei Plekhanov, York University

Russia's foreign policies since the fall of the USSR have been evolving under the influence of two basic imperatives: the imperative of systemic transformation and the imperative of geopolitical position. The requirements of Russia's systemic transformation into a capitalist-type society (the market imperative) and the realities of her historic-geographic position as Eurasia's core state (the geopolitical imperative) may interact in a number of ways.

They can be mutually reinforcing, making it possible to achieve significant foreign policy gains. They can be mutually exclusive, forcing Russia's leaders to make hard choices between them, which makes policy setbacks likely. And they can be managed through tradeoffs, which, of course, requires great political skills, significant and diverse power resources, and effective institutions.

There is also the question of choices and balances between market and geopolitical considerations in Russia's international behaviour. If the market imperative is considered decisive, Russia can be expected to try to market its geopolitical assets – that is, to achieve economic gains through a skillful use of its unique geopolitical position. Alternatively, if the geopolitical imperative becomes uppermost in foreign policy, Russia may adopt mercantilist stances and use market interactions with other countries to achieve maximum possible geopolitical gains. Needless to say, different forces within Russia favour different market-geopolitical balances.

Generally speaking, post-communist Russia's foreign policy is conservative, cautious and pragmatic, serving as a stabilizing factor in an international situation characterized by high degrees of tension and unpredictability.

Russian Foreign Policy Constants

POST-COMMUNIST ECUMENISM. Despite the disappearance of the USSR with its global ideological claims, Russia remains a state on a par only with the United States in terms of the breadth of its geopolitical interests, which continue to involve Russia in nearly every major international issue which exists today. The geopolitical factor, reinforced by the factor of nuclear parity, contributes to the maintenance of the US-Russian axis as one of the most important bilateral relationships in the post-post-Cold War world. But geopolitics also makes it imperative for the Russian state, and for Russia's political and economic elites, to pursue active policies in all directions. It would be imprudent for Russia to develop its partnership with the US, for instance, at the expense of her relations with China, or to participate in the 'antiterrorist coalition' in ways which could alienate Russia from the Islamic world.

THE POWER GAP. Russia's real (usable) power in world politics is, of course, limited out of proportion to the breadth of Russia's global interests. This power gap compels Russian elites to act with caution and pragmatism (in particular, Russia cannot afford to have strong enemies anywhere). But the mismatch between needs and resources may create vacuums and situations of overextension, pregnant with potential for policy blunders.

THE PRIMACY OF ECONOMICS. Russia's foremost foreign policy interests lie in the economic sphere: struggle for markets, achieving successful integration into the global economy, and a revival of Russia's national economy on a capitalist basis. This orientation is underpinned by the interests of Russia's post-communist elites, determined to secure and enhance their gains of the past decade, and to seek business opportunities in every part of the world.

THE INSTITUTIONAL DEFICIT. Given the insifficient institutionalization of Russia's political system, the process of foreign policy making is characterized, on the one hand, by the absolute primacy of the President, and, on the other hand, by uncertainty with regard to his actual control over the implementation of his decisions. In a highly institutionalized democracy, effective pluralism in the making of a decision gives way to effective, streamlined process of implementation of the decision which has been made. In the Russian case, the ability of the President to make decisions without broad and structured consultations is accompanied by the ability of bureaucratic and business elites to distort and even sabotage the President's chosen course.

The Two Transitions

In the past few years, a new relationship began to form between Russia and the US, as part of the process of the political transitions taking place in the two countries

In Russia, the transition from Yeltsin to Putin signified the beginning of restoration of a strong state. Stabilization of the Russian domestic scene has been accompanied by an economic recovery and the promotion of a neoliberal economic reform agenda. Russia no longer looks like a basket case as it did throughout the 1990s. Whether or not these trends should hold for long, there is a new and growing global perception that Russia seems to have begun to recover from its prolonged transition crisis through reliance on a combination of capitalist economics and a reasserted political authoritarianism. In the area of foreign policy, the formation of the Putin coalition has symbolized the emergence of a new pragmatic consensus between Western-oriented and Eurasianist-oriented elites.

The transition from Clinton to Bush, which came on the heels of the Russian transition, had important political implications for Russia. On the one hand, the emergence of a colder, more unilateralist and potentially more dangerous America did present a serious challenge to

Russia's interests and thus generated alarmed reactions in Moscow. On the other hand, as a result of the two transitions an unusual ideological affinity arose between the dominant mindsets in Moscow and Washington: commitment to laissez-faire economics, emphasis on geopolitics, and a stronger assertion of national interests (in the US case, as a manifestation of strength, in the Russian case, as a function of weakness). And the end of the Clinton-era micromanagement of Russian reforms allowed the Russians to feel a little more in control of their country's policies than they did in the 1990s.

As the weaker party, more concerned about the deterioration of relations between the two countries than President Bush, President Putin actively sought a new dialog with the new US Administration, and, after a few setbacks, achieved success. Months before 9/11, the Bush Administration's initial attitude of neglect of (and near-contempt for) Russia began to give way to a growing perception of Russia's potential usefulness to the US. The Bush-Putin summits in Genoa and Ljubljana signified the start of a new partnership. Without those summits, Putin's reaction to 9/11 might have been different.

Different Readings of the Post-9/11 Balance Sheet

As noted by many analysts, Russia benefited from the events of September 11 in a number of ways:

1. The attack, with its implications of a wider global conflict between the West and Islamist radicalism, highlighted Russia's vital geopolitical role. Russia's stability, security and strength (both economic and military) became important international concerns.

2. In the post-9/11 situation, the US found itself in dire need of allies in the new global confrontation. In at least two important respects, Russia became more important to the US as an ally than NATO or Japan: a) successful US operations in Eurasia require Russia's cooperation and help; and b) Russia may serve as an important alternative supplier of energy to the US in case of disruption of supplies from the Persian Gulf.

3. Putin's early focus on the global threat of Islamist terrorism was to some extent vindicated. After 9/11, what looked in 1999 as a crude attempt to justify Russia's crackdown in Chechnya began to look as a realistic threat assessment. This took some international pressure off Russia's Chechnya operations.

4. The refocusing of US foreign policy on the war on Islamist terrorism has partly relieved the geopolitical pressures Moscow had felt before 9/11, when many in Russia's foreign policy elite were inclined to see the 'Western threat' (NATO expansion, the New Great Game over Caspian oil, etc.) compounded by 'the Islamist threat' to Russia's interests in the Caucasus and Central Asia.

5. Russia has gained a voice in NATO, an official status of a market economy, an upgrading of her status in G8, and support for her entry into WTO.

6. Joining the US in the 'antiterrorist coalition', Russia in her new role as a key US ally has gained some freedom to pursue its own interests in other areas (including its relations with countries like Iran and North Korea, regarded by the US as 'rogue states').

7. The political climate for Western investments in Russia and for Russian business activities in the West has improved.

8. The new conservative security mindset, characterizing the Bush Administration after 9/11, is consonant with the political orientations of Russian leaders and the traditions of the Russian state.

9. Rearmament of Russia, viewed as essential and urgent by all Russian elites, can now be legitimized in the eyes of the US and other leading powers much more effectively than before.

10. Improvement of Russia's relations with the US is supported by most Russian elites and a majority of the population, which is an important political asset for Putin and his coalition.

Indeed, by joining 'the anti-terror coalition', Russia has been able to make gains across a wide and diverse spectrum of issues. But these gains have entailed some costs. Russia's main costs have involved acquiescence with what looked unacceptable before 9/11: NATO's massive expansion eastwards, America's pullout from arms control, direct US security involvement across the belt of post-Soviet states from the Baltic to Pamir, and Russia's decision to withdraw from key Cold War military bases in Southeast Asia and the Caribbean. In case of US military occupation of Iraq, Russia will be pressured to acquiesce with even more: establishment of direct US control over the Persian Gulf and its energy resources.

The questions Putin's critics (and allies, too) have raised with regard to this new situation, focus on the price Russia has paid and the value it has bought. Has the post-9/11 deal been fair for Russia? Has Russia lost more than it gained by this acquiescence? Are the gains largely symbolic and/or transitory, while the losses are tangible and lasting? These questions are potentially dangerous for Putin in the Russian political context.

From the perspective of Russia's traditionalists, conservatives, and so-called 'Eurasianists' (it is misleading to tag all of them as unreconstructed communists because their defining characteristic is not communism but Russian nationalism), Russia has come out, at least so far, as a clear loser from its new strategic partnership with the US. From this perspective, what is happening is nothing less than Russia's retreat in the face of a vigorous American offensive.

The notion of a retreat is steeped in geopolitical thinking, which in the days of the Clinton Administration was sneered at as 'old think'. But today, it is remarkable that most of the discourse on the question of Russia's gains and losses since 9/11 has taken place in a geopolitical frame of reference (which is just one of many signs that at the dawn of the 21st century, geopolitics is back with a vengeance, even if in modernized forms).

Indeed, when Russia is praised in the West, and criticized in China and in Russian conservative circles, for not objecting to American deployments in the post-Soviet South, the inevitable major inference is that the Russian acquiescence is, indeed, of major political importance. If we grant that Russia's own weight in international politics has grown largely due to the increased salience and significance of geopolitics, then we have to grant that Russia's acquiescence was a very high price to pay. Few would argue that a retreat has not taken place, and that this is Russia's price for its closer integration with the West. The debates, both within Russia and internationally, are about what this retreat means.

The best-case interpretation comes from Russia's Westernizers, who argue that Russia has gained massively because it is now much more closely identified and tied with the West than at any time since the fall of the Romanovs. But even the Westernizers feel compelled to address the geopolitical aspects of the process, and they offer the following points:

> 1. The new American presence in Central Eurasia represents Russia's gain, not a loss, inasmuch as it strengthens Russia's security in areas of Russia's vulnerability: in the face of the current threat from radical Islamism and of the future potential threat of Chinese expansionism.

> 2. To try to resist the American thrust is imprudently risky for Russia, given the huge usable-power disparity between the two sides.

3. The Americans are unlikely to stay in the post-Soviet South for long. Their presence will inevitably generate discontent and opposition which will ultimately result in their pullout, and Russia will have a chance to return to fill the void. In order to make it happen, Russia must be careful not to alienate the Americans, while at the same time maintaining its own distinct role.

4. In the new common cause between Russia and the West, NATO's expansion is not a cause for alarm; indeed, it is possible to view it as a process leading up to Russia's future membership in the Western alliance.

5. To the Americans, the Westernizers present a bill for Russia's huge geopolitical concessions. Their complaint that the payment has been meager is only partly a bargaining ploy: underlying the complaint is the fear that the deal may really not have been very good for Russia.

According to the worst-case view, propagated vigorously by Russia's conservative nationalists, the power predominance of the United States is so huge that Russia is highly unlikely to reap any benefits from its new partnership.

1. Russia cannot possibly compete with the US on market terms. In any kind of an open market relationship between the two sides, America's global economic hegemony will guarantee that the US will always be the dominant partner, dictating the terms and reaping most benefits, while Russia will have to accept a subordinate, dependent, almost colonial status.

2. Russia should use its geopolitical assets, but not by selling them.

3. Russia should vigorously pursue integration with its post-Soviet neighbours and rebuff Western attempts to establish permanent positions in post-Soviet territories.

4. America respects only strength. Russia will be able to make serious, durable gains in international politics only if it works to restore, in one way or another, to one extent or another, a balance of power vis-à-vis the United States.

5. To turn Russia into the West's ally against China and the Islamic world (distinction between Islam and Islamism is usually blurred in this argument) would expose Russia's security to great dangers. Russia should align with China and Islamic states in order to resist American hegemony.

What underlies the arguments of the Westernizers is the notion of Russian-Western ('Euro-Atlantic') solidarity based on both market and geopolitical considerations. What underlies the Eurasianists' arguments is the unreconstructed "realist" view of world politics, where Russia is paying dearly for its lingering liberal-internationalist illusions which have already led her to a historic geopolitical defeat.

It is hard for the Westernizers to win the debate, if only because they agree with the Eurasianists on some of the most important points in the latter's position. Not only they have to argue within a geopolitical frame of reference, which the Eurasianists insist upon – but also, when they argue within a market frame of reference, they have to recognize the weakness of Russia's market assets in a highly competitive global economy. Westernizers' case for a market-geopolitical synthesis is easy to present as unrealistic, based on wishful thinking. The Eurasianist case for the unquestioned dominance of the geopolitical imperative which should determine Russia's economic strategies often seems more fitting for a world which has left the decade of liberal hopes and entered the period of a new war.

Is An Effective Synthesis Possible?

Putin desperately seeks to integrate elements of Westernizer and Eurasianist approaches in a pragmatic foreign policy course. He tries to make the most of Russia's unique geography. He impresses the Europeans from Blair to Berlusconi with his apparently genuine commitment to making Russia an integral part of Europe. To the Chinese, the Indians, the Koreans and other Asians, he presents Russia as a major Asian power which can be of great use to Asia in a lot of ways. To the Americans, he presents Russia as the other end of an important world power axis, except this time Russia offers itself not as the sworn global enemy, as in the Cold War, but as a key partner in 'the Euroatlantic Comminity', stretching from Vancouver to Vladivostok. Just wait till he goes on an African tour.

In his programmatic statements on Russian foreign policy, Putin reiterates that the global economy is a highly competitive place where Russia cannot expect any favours and must fight hard for a decent 'place under economic sun'. Russia's integration is portrayed as a hard-nosed, pragmatic choice: unless Russia is a full-fledged participant among those who make rules for the global economy, those rules will be more detrimental to Russia's interests. Russia must join in order to be able to compete with everybody else more successfully. If Gorbachev and Yeltsin borrowed money from the West, Putin is repaying the debts ahead of schedule. This type of foreign policy has overwhelming support in Russia.

In a sense, Putin's foreign policy course treats Russia's geopolitical assets primarily as commodities to be used to gain Russia maximum access to world markets. But, since Russia needs these assets for its security, as well, the real issue in the post-9/11 bargaining between Bush and Putin is whether Russia is selling – or merely leasing. As only time will tell, of course.

The key issue, then, is how successful Russia will be in marketing its geopolitics. If it is successful, then Russia will continue on its Westernizing course. If not, it may be forced to revert to some variety of protectionist Eurasianism, putting geopolitical priorities ahead of its quest of a decent "place under the economic sun".

Russia emerged from that fight as a key player in international efforts to contain American unilateralism. Coordinating its diplomacy with two other UNSC Permanent Members, France and China, Russia opposed a specific US policy option, pushed by a specific group within the US Government, thus enhancing the position of another group. In a real sense, Russia's diplomacy became a factor influencing US policy-making to help bring about a US policy Russia could support.

In the world after September 11, Russia's potential as a relatively independent actor in world politics is higher than is assumed by those who cite its power gap and its institutional deficit. Still, the gap and the deficit are glaring realities. What has given Russia a heightened international role is the new war – 'war on terror'. But a new war is the last thing Russia needs if it wants to build a viable, competitive market economy and an efficient democratic state. In case this war escalates, Russia may be forced by the logic of events to revert to its habitual mode of existence: an armed camp controlling the heart of Eurasia – hardly a prospect anyone would welcome.[1]

Notes

[1] The following sources were used:

Vladimir Abarinov, Shirok russkij chelovek, ya by suzil, *Grani.ru*, 23.08.2002, <http://www.grani.ru/us_rf/articles/rf_execution/> (in Russian);

"Amerika menyaet otnoshenie k Rossii posle Nord-Osta". *Nezavisimaya gazeta*. 4.11.2002 (in Russian);

Alexei Andreev, Voyna s Irakom veroyatna na 70%. Rossiya predostavila amerikantsam polnuyu svobodu deistvij, *Nezavisimaya gazeta*, 6.12.2002 (in Russian);

Alexei Arbatov, Interview, *Ekho Moskvy*, 4.10.2001 (in Russian);

Stephen Blank, "Russia and the U.S. War on Terrorism", in: *Defeating Terrorism: Strategic Issue Analyses*, ed, Colonel John R. Martin, U.S. Army War College. Strategic Studies Institute, January 2002;

Maxim Blant, Prezident Jekyll i podpolkovnik Hyde, *Ezhenedel'nyj zhurnal*, 21.07.02 (in Russian);

Alexei Bolotnikov, Rumsfeld raskritikoval Rossiyu, *Nezavisimaya gazeta*, 23.08.2002 (in Russian);

Zbigniew Brzezinski, Extracts from Living With Russia, *The National Interest*, No. 61, Fall 2000;

Zbigniew Brzezinski, *The Grand Chessboard. American Primacy and Its Geostrategic Imperatives* (Basic Books, 1997);

Georgi Bulychev and Alexandr Vorontsov, Severokorejskij pasjans, *Nezavisimaya gazeta*, 26.08.2002 (in Russian);

"Busha ne udastsya pereigrat'", *Gazeta.ru*, 15.04.2002 <http://www.gazeta.ru/print/2002/04/15/bushneud.shtml> (in Russian);

"Can Russia handle a changed world?" *The Economist*, September 1-7, 2001;

"Central Asia. Back into the cauldron." *The Economist*, September 5-11, 2002;

Charles Clover, "Will the Russian Bear Roar Again?" *Financial Times*, 2 December 2000;

Michael Croissant and Bulent Aras, *Oil and Geopolitics in the Caspian Sea Region*, (Praeger, 2000);

Georgi Derluguian, *Putin in Russian Historical Context*, Program on New Approaches to Russian Security Policy Memo Series, Series Editor, Erin Powers, Memo No.112. <http://www.fas.harvard.edu/~poars/POLICY%20MEMOS/Derluguian112>;

Georgi Derluguian, *Anti-Americanism on the Rise? Suggestions Toward a Rational Program of Study.* October 2002, PONARS Policy Memo No. 266 <http://www.csis.org/ruseura/ponars/policymemos/pm_index.htm>;

Robert H.Donaldson and Joseph Nogee, *The Foreign Policy of Russia: Changing Systems, Enduring Interests*, (M.E.Sharpe, 1998);

Gregory Feifer, "Putin's Foreign Policy a Private Affair", *Moscow Times*, April 2, 2002;

David Filipov, "Putin, pursuing status, is seen lacking a policy. Priorities called practical, if fuzzy", *Boston Globe*, March 13, 2001;

Dmitry Furman, Polyot dvuglavogo oral, *Obshchaya gazeta*, 30.05.2002 (in Russian);

Alexandr Golts, Diplomatiya spetsnaznachentsev, *Yezhenedel'nyj zhurnal*, 23. 07.2002, <http://ej.ru/028/life/01column/index.html> (in Russian);

Thomas Graham, "Let's have a Real Debate about Policy toward Russia", *Christian Science Monitor*, October 26, 2000;

William Anthony Hay, "America, Europe, and Russia: Bush's Search for Common Ground. Foreign Policy Research Institute", *Watch on the West*, 3.7, June 2002, <www.fpri.org>;

Fiona Hill, "Extremists and Bandits: How Russia Views the War against Terrorism", PONARS Policy Memo No. 246 – April 2002;

Ted Hopf, ed, *Understandings of Russian Foreign Policy*, (Pennsylvania State U. Press, 1999);

Evelyn Iritani and John Daniszewski, "Economic stakes are high as the five key Security Council members discussing a military strike on Baghdad eye its reserves", *Los Angeles Times*, November 5, 2002;

I.S. Ivanov, Traditsii rossijskoj diplomaticheskoj shkoly. *Mezhdunarodnaya zhizn'*, June 2002 (in Russian);

Leonid Ivashov, NATO priobretaet novoye kachestvo. – *NVO*, 29.11.2002 (in Russian);

Johnson's Russia List. Washington, Center for Defense Information, 2001-2002 (Listserv: <davidjohnson@erols.com>, A CDI Project, <www.cdi.org>);

Robert G. Kaiser, "U.S. Plants Footprint in Shaky Central Asia", *The Washington Post*, August 27, 2002;

Charles W. Kegley and Gregory Raymond, *A Multipolar Peace? Great-Power Politics in the Twenty-First Century*, (St.Martin's Press, 1994);

Anatoly Kostyukov, Zyuganov predupredil prezidenta ob ugroze s Zapada. Putin vryad li primet yego soviety, *Nezavisimaya gazeta*, 19.11.2002 (in Russian);

John P. LeDonne, *The Russian Empire and the World, 1700-1917. The Geopolitics of Expansion and Containment* (Oxford U. Press, 1997);

Robert Legvold, "Russia's Unformed Foreign Policy", *Foreign Affairs*, September/October 2001;

Anatol Lieven, "Russia and Realpolitik: Western Europe must forge a pragmatic relationship with Russia rather than treat it as an errant child", *Financial Times* (UK), October 3, 2001;

V.B. Lukov, Na Zapade mnogie s udivleniem otkryli dlya sebya nezamenimuyu rol' Rossii. *Mezhdunarodnaya zhizn'*, December 2001 (in Russian);

Neil Malcolm, Alex Pravda, Roy Allison, and Margot Light, *Internal Factors in Russian Foreign Policy*, (Oxford U. Press, 1996);

Michael Mandelbaum, ed, *The New Russian Foreign Policy*, (New York: Council on Foreign Relations, 1998);

Sergey Markov, Yesli ne Putin i Bush – to Ben Laden, *Strana.ru*, 20.05.2002. <http://www.grani.ru/nukes/articles/start3/> (in Russian);

Roy Medvedev, Vladimir Putin – deistvuyushchij president, Moskva: Vremya, 2002 (in Russian);

Yekaterina Milovanova, Rossiyu zavalyat zakazami na vooruzheniya. *Utro.ru*, 22.08.2001. <http://www.utro.ru/articles/2001082202171431170.shtml> (in Russian);

"Mir i Rossiya na poroge XXI veka. Vtorye gorchakovskie chteniya. MGIMO MID Rossii (23-24 maya 2000 g.) Moskva: ROSSPEN, 2001 (in Russian);

Arkady Teplo Orlov, eshche teplee, *Ezhenedel'nyj zhurnal*, 21.05.2002 (in Russian);

"Perekhod k novym otnosheniyam mezhdu Vostokom i Zapadom. Rezul'taty tryokhstoronnego obsuzhdeniya. Doklad Rabochej gruppy po obsuzhdeniyu otnoshenij Rossiya-NATO". Atlantic Council of the USA, Moscow Carnegie Center, Center for Eropean Reform, Institute of the USA and Canada of the Russian Academy of Sciences. Moscow, April 12, 2002 (in Russian);

Scott Peterson, "US-Russia ties jolted by crisis in Georgia", *The Christian Science Monitor*, August 26, 2002;

William Pfaff, "Controlling the Caucasus. Putin's 'war on terrorism' outmaneuvers the U.S", *International Herald Tribune*, October 31, 2002;

Andrei Piontkovsky, Vstrecha na Elbe-2. Novaya gazeta, 21.10.2002 (in Russian);

"Press Briefing on President Bush's Upcoming Summit Meeting with Vladmir Putin", Council on Foreign Relations, May 14, 2002, Washington, DC. *Johnson's Russia List* #6252, 18 May 2002, <davidjohnson@erols.com>, a CDI Project, <www.cdi.org>;

Yevgenii Primakov, Vosem' mesyatsev plius... Moscow, "Mysl'", 2001 (in Russian);

"Putin issues decree to freeze terrorists' assets, block funding", *BBC Monitoring Service* – United Kingdom; April 18, 2002;

"Putin tells journalists of human rights in Chechnya and freedom of media", Text of report by Russian Public TV on 7 April. *BBC Monitoring Service* – United Kingdom; April 7, 2002;

Phil Reeves, "Putin brings offer of nuclear-tipped arms deal to India", *The Independent*, December 5, 2002;

Rossijskaya demokraticheskaya partiya "Yabloko". Federal'nyj soviet. Rezoliutsiya "O vneshnej politike Rossijskoj Federatsii". 15.06.2002. <http://www.yabloko.ru/Press/Docs/2002/0615fs-resol-vneshpolit.html >(in Russian);

"RFE/RL Business Watch", Radio Free Europe-Radio Liberty, Prague, 2001-2002;

Tatiana Rublyova, Proshchaj, Kavkaz! SshA nachinajut operatsiyu po vytesneniyu Rossii. *Nezavisimaya gazeta*, 27.08.2002 (in Russian);

"Russia's Iraq Stance May Force Intervention By Blair", *Stratfor.com*, October 2, 2002;

"Russia's overseas investment: Comrade capitalist", *The Economist*, February 15, 2001;

Dimitri K. Simes, *After the Collapse: Russia Seeks Its Place As a Great Power*, (Simon and Schuster, 1999);

Leonid Slutsky, Mify i real'nosti. *Izvestiya*, 3.11.2002 (in Russian); Vladislav Smolentsev, Rossiya, Hande hoch! (My uzhe ne khozyaeva v sobstvennom dome), *Zavtra,* 12.11.2002 (in Russian);

Flemming Splitsboel-Hansen, "Past and Future Meet: Aleksandr Gorchakov and Russian Foreign Policy", *Europe-Asia Studies*, 54.3 (2002)377-396;

"Stenogramma press-konferentsii Ministra inostrannykh del Rossii I.S. Ivanova v informagentstve "Interfax" 18 oktyabrya 2002 goda". 2145-19-10-2002, Ministry of Foreign Affairs of the Russian Federation, 19.10.2002 (in Russian);

"The Foreign Policy Concept of the Russian Federation. Approved by the President of the Russian Federation V.Putin", Moscow: Kremlin, June 28, 2000;

"Topical Aspects of Russian Foreign Policy" Article of Russian Deputy Foreign Minister Alexei Meshkov, published in Mezhdunarodnaya Zhizn Magazine, No. 4, 2002, 778-18-04-2002, Ministry of Foreign Affairs of the Russian Federation, 18.04.2002;

"Transcript of Russian Foreign Minister Igor Ivanov Remarks at Meeting of Supervisory Council for Development of the International Institute of the Fuel and Energy Complex at the Russian MFA's MGIMO(U), March 14, 2002". 469-15-03-2002 Ministry of Foreign Affairs of the Russian Federation, Mar 18, 2002 Ian Traynor, "Kremlin gives short shrift to US hawk over Iraq", *The Guardian*, September 12, 2002;

Henry Trofimenko, Tsarskoe Selo, kovbojskoye sedlo… *Zavtra*, 12.11.2002 (in Russian);

Henry Trofimenko, *Russian National Interests and the Current Crisis in Russia*, (Ashgate, 1999);

Astrid Tuminez, *Russian Nationalism Since 1856: Ideology and the Making of Foreign Policy*, (Rowman and Littlefield, 2000);

Ole Tunander, Pavel Baev and Victoria Einagel *Geopolitics in Post-Wall Europe: Security, Territory and Identity*, (Sage, 1997);

Patrick Tyler, "In Russia's Expanded World Order, Putin Courts Allies Old and New", *The New York Times*, December 12, 2000;

Vystuplenie Prezidenta Rossijskoj Federatsii V.V.Putina v Bundestage FRG, 25.09.2001.<http://www.president.kremlin.ru/text/appears/2001/09/10456> (in Russian);

Vystuplenie Prezidenta Rossijskoj Federatsii V.V.Putina na rasshirennom soveshchanii s uchastiem poslov Rossiiskoj Federatsii v MID Rossii. 12.07.2002.<http://www.president.kremlin.ru/withflash/appears/2002/07/12.sht ml> (in Russian);

Celeste Wallander, ed, *The Sources of Russian Foreign Policy After the Cold War*, (Boulder: Westview Press, 1996);

Joby Warrick, "U.S. weighs moves on uranium sites in 16 nations", *The Washington Post,* August 2, 2002;

Mark Webber, *Russia and Europe: Conflict or Cooperation?* (Palgrave, 2000);

Stephen A. Weisman, "How Powell Lined Up Votes, Starting With His President's", *The New York Times,* November 9, 2002; and

"What Russia wants: Vladimir Putin's long, hard haul", *The Economist*, May 16, 2002.

Eurasianism in Russian Foreign Policy

Eugene Kvache, Undergraduate Student, York University

---

*"By its very nature Eurasia is historically
destined to comprise a single state entity".*
N. Trubetskoi[1]

Russia's national identity has long been a subject of numerous scholarly discussions in both Russian and foreign academic circles. Primarily, Russia's uniqueness stems from the geographical factors, as it is the largest country in the world stretching across Europe and Asia. Reflections on the fate of Russia have been especially intense during transition periods in her tumultious history. In the contemporary period, characterized by the disappearence of the Soviet Union and the whithering away of the official communist ideology, a vacuum has emerged, which calls for new ideas to help Russia overcome the massive challenges of the post-communist transition and to regain the position that it once enjoyed on the world stage.

One of the ideas which have gained prominence is the concept of Eurasianism. Its history dates back to the stormy debates between 'Westernizers' and 'Slavophiles' which raged in Russia in mid-nineteenth century. While the Westernizers insisted that the only way to successfully modernize Russia was the European model, the Slavophiles viewed Russia as the 'Third Rome', distinct from Europe and destined to create and lead a new, more spiritual Slavic civilization.

Eurasianism is also closely connected with geopolitical thought, popularized at the beginning of the twentieth century by British geographer Sir Halford Mackinder, Admiral T. Mahan of the US Navy, and others. According to Mackinder and his followers, a kind of natural global cleavage exists in world politics between land powers and sea powers. In this model, the natural repository for global land power is the Eurasian Heartland, the bulk of which was occupied for several centuries by the Russian empire. Whoever controls the heartland, wrote Mackinder, will forever seek to dominate the Eurasian landmass and ultimately the world.[2]

In its benign form, Eurasianism simply restates Russia's uniqueness and argues that Russia can take up a position of world rank and prestige without copying the Western model. Eurasianists of more extreme persuasions view the Eurasian Heartland through a 'Clash of Civilizations' prism, as the base of a global anti-Western crusade whose goal is the ultimate expulsion of 'Atlantic' (read: 'American') influence from the continent.

The goal of this paper is to outline the development of Eurasianist thought from its origins to the present day and to evaluate its impact on the contemporary Russian foreign policy discourse.

The Slavophile-Westernizer Debate in the Middle of the 19th Century

The Slavophile-Westernizer debate is rooted in the history of Russia since 1700s. Peter the Great's reforms brought Russia out of the cultural isolation and stimulated the growth of the educated elite consisting of nobility and the petty service class. The Napoleonic wars of the early nineteenth century brought this educated elite into contact with the ideas of the French revolution, informing some of these young officers to call for reform and liberalization and eventually stage the Decembrist uprising of 1825. The reactionary policies adopted by Tsar Nicholas I in response to the revolt generated profound frustration and dissatisfaction among the educated elite. In that atmosphere, an intense intellectual debate erupted, concerning the very fundamentals of Russian history, Russia's place in Europe, and the paths of future development of the country.

A catalyst for the debate was a book by Pyotr Chaadaev, titled *Philosophical Letters* and published in 1836. Chaadaev wrote about Russia's cultural isolation and backwardness, arguing that Russia had no past, present or future and had contributed nothing to world culture. According to Chaadaev, Russia had been shut out of the mainstream of history by Russian Orthodox religion, which encouraged a retreat from the world. Western culture, meanwhile, had benefited from the spirit underlying Western churches, which encouraged involvement in ethical and social issues of the time. Chaadaev was critical of Peter the Great's efforts to Westernize Russia, arguing that he had failed to civilize, providing instead only a superficial veneer of Westernization through imitation and importation. Chaadaev saw the value of Russian historical experience exclusively in demonstrating to the rest of the world the frightening lesson of complete exclusion from the global spiritual unity.[3]

Chaadaev's writings stimulated the growth of Westernizer thought. Key members were philosopher Herzen and historian Timofei Granovskiy, who was teaching at the Department of General History at the Moscow University. The West was the source of their inspiration, not so much because there they saw complete perfection in the Western model, but because they considered it as a more 'cultured', more progressive way of life. It was in the West that the beneficial fruits of Enlightenment were enjoyed at their fullest by the society.

However, the Westernizers did not advocate slavish copying of all things Western. This was evidenced in the writings of another leading Westenizer, Belinskiy: "It is time for us to cease admiring everything European simply because it is not Asiatic and to admire, respect, and seek it simply because it is 'human', rejecting on those grounds everything European that is not human as vigorously as we would reject everything Asiatic that is not human".[4]

Above all, the Westernizers upheld the ideals of personal liberty and social freedom as essential conditions for the development of Russia. However, while some found that woes of Russia were due to 'insufficient' westernization, others saw them as a result of the 'excessive' westernization. This pattern of thought was termed 'Slavophile' and was touted as the alternative to the Westernizers.

The Slavophiles, led by Alexei Khomiakov and Ivan Kireevsky, felt that Russia should follow its own path, one based on the superior values and principles embodied in Russian Orthodoxy and expressed in institutions such as the family and the peasant commune. According to the Slavophiles, the Orthodox Church consisted of a congregation of individuals who, renouncing personal egoism and individuality, voluntarily entered into an organic union based on love, common faith, customs and values. Individuals became part of a greater whole and shared in a wisdom and spiritual truth that could be found only in the Church.

Such ideal social bonds contrasted with those present in the West, according to the Slavophiles. The West embodied individualism and rationalism, where individuals were bound together not by a community of moral values but by contracts, interests and laws that demanded obedience. The Slavophiles argued that the problems of the West such as social conflict and isolation of the individual from the society were rooted in the Western Church, where external authority replaced a free and organic union. The Slavophiles believed that during Peter the Great's reign such an organic relationship had been destroyed, as the government had invaded the people's domain.[5]

At the heart of the Westernizer-Slavophile debate was the fundamental issue: What is Russia's role in history? While the Westernizers answered that Russia could play an important historical role only if it followed the path that Peter the Great had prescribed, Slavophiles answered that Russia could aspire to a great role in the future only if it stayed true to its unique traditions and avoided excessive westernization. This debate flared up in new forms and with new intensity in the 20th century.

Eurasianism After the Russian Revolution

The internal contradictions of the Russian Empire were resolved, for better or worse, in the revolutions of 1917 that brought an end to the tsarist regime. A large number of Russian intellectuals chose to flee Russia in the face of the Bolshevik victory. Eurasianism emerged as an ideological trend in the 1920s among Russian emigrates abroad. Their isolation from the homeland along with an acute sense of catastrophic character of the changes generated by the First World War and the revolution in Russia, served as a strong stimulus for the attempts of the exiles to understand their lot. The futility of overcoming Bolshevism by means of weapons being obvious in the 1920s, it led to setting the goal of overcoming it spiritually. Previous ideological approaches seemed inadequate under those conditions and required total innovation. It was the Eurasianist who made an attempt at such innovation.

Eurasianism was heavily influenced by geopolitical theoreticians like Danilevsky and Mackinder. Mackinder held that the "Eurasian Heartland", spanning across Europe and Asia, had natural and climatic features which had shaped the common characteristics of economic, cultural and political development of the peoples living there. Its geographic integrity with the steppe as a common factor determined the unity of their historical development and ethno-psychological features, religious beliefs and languages which were formed under the influence of the environment.

According to Nikolai Trubetzkoy, one of the founders of Eurasianism, the origins of the Eurasian identity dated back not to Kievan Rus, but rather to the Empire of Genghis Khan, which played an important role in the state formation of Muscovite Russia and preserved the Russian Orthodox Church under the conditions of religious and military threat from the 'Latin West'. The Moscow State became the direct successor of the Empire. Thus, the Eurasians considered the nomadic peoples to be an active subject of the Russian historical process and evaluated the impact of the 'Tartar yoke' as positive at least to some extent.[6]

In the view of the Eurasianists, the westernization of Russia, started by Peter the Great and continued by his successors, resulted in distorting Russia's Eurasian originality and contaminating the national self-consciousness of the intelligentsia who uncritically adopted Western patterns.[7] This led to a cultural split between the lower and upper classes and eventually resulted in the 1917 revolution. But the raging revolutionary storm contributed to freeing Russia's Eurasian essence from the superficial European touch. According to the Eurasianist historians, the future was to reveal Russia-Eurasia global mission: to become the center of attraction for non-European peoples in the struggle between the West and the East.

The Eurasianists, sharing a "catastrophic perception" of the ongoing global changes, strove for a new understanding of the cultural-historical ideal that was to become a foundation for the spiritual overcoming of Bolshevism. It was supposed to be based on the notions of Russia as a great-power, nationalist Orthodox state.[8]

The concept of 'Moscow as the Third Rome', and thus the guardian of Christian Orthodoxy, fitted perfectly in this perspective. Having borrowed this idea from the Slavophiles, the Eurasianists adapted it to modern conditions. Messianism was another characteristic feature of Eurasianist thinking. According to them, a special mission had been predetermined by Providence and by historical fate for the Russian people. The mission was to show the world the way out of the global crisis unleashed by the world war.[9] Eurasianist ideas were destined to remain without practical applications to reality until the collapse of the Soviet Union.

Eurasianism in Post-Communist Russia

With the fall of Communism, geopolitics came to be regarded as an important frame of reference for foreign policy makers. Andrei Kozyrev, Russia's foreign minister in the early 1990's, stated barely a month after the dissolution of the Soviet Union, "We rapidly come to understand that geopolitics ... is replacing [the communist] ideology".[10]

After the end of the Cold War and the dissolution of the USSR, Russia found itself in a new international situation. It was reduced in geographic size. While a number of important seaports and military bases were lost, there appeared an enclave of the Kaliningrad Region, isolated from Russia by Belarus and Lithuania. Further, Russia was deprived of her Warsaw Pact allies in Eastern and Central Europe, while obtaining along its new 'transparent' boundaries a number of states with unfriendly governments (especially in the Baltic States).

Faced with these challenges in the early 1990s, Russian foreign policy makers conceptually divided Russia's international environment into two zones. Former republics of the Soviet Union were termed to be the 'near abroad', while the rest of the world was the 'far abroad'. In the euphoria of the early post-Soviet years, many Russian diplomats wishfully thought that the former Soviet republics, grateful to Moscow for their freedom and sharing the same past, would opt for the retention of 'fraternal bonds' with the Russian metropole.[11] Also, there were the hopes that with end of the 'Cold War' the West would become for new

Russia a reliable political ally, a generous donor, and an ideal model for imitation in matters of social and economic development. Needless to say, none of these hopes have materialized in its entirety.

In the aftermath of the loss of prestige on the world stage, Eurasianist thinking provided an attractive alternative model for Russia. Eurasianism was capturing the imagination of members of the Russian political elite, and today counts many adherents at the top levels of Russian policy-makers. They range from such figures as the leader of the Communist Party, which is by far the largest political organization in Russia today. Gennadi Zyuganov, its chairman, has published a geopolitical manifesto, The Geography of Victory, in which he abandoned anything resembling traditional communist doctrine. "We live in an era where geopolitics is literally knocking at the door, and ignoring it would be not just a mistake, but a crime", stated Zyuganov in the introduction to his manifesto.[12] Some commentators found Eurasianist sympathies in the policies of Russia's Prime Minister Yevgeni Primakov. His policies fitted the Eurasianist doctrine so neatly that it was hard not to view Primakov as one of the movement's backers, although he has never publicly stated his position on the theory.[13]

One of the primary proponents of Eurasianism in modern Russia is an increasingly influential former historian Aleksandr Dugin. He has updated Eurasianism by dropping its initial postulate about the eternal hostility of Russia and the West as a whole. Instead, he speaks about the concentration of what he calls 'the world evil' in the major naval powers of the West – Great Britain and the United States. He argues that Russia should form an alliance with continental Europe against those Atlantic powers, an alliance which would seek both ideological and geoeconomic dominance in world affairs. According to Dugin, the economic strength of the naval powers is based on their control of the oceans. In response, Russia should lead Eurasia in creating east-west and north-south land transport networks.[14]

Finally, there was a widespread feeling that the pro-Western approach to foreign policy had overestimated the 'commonality of interests' between Russia and the Euro-Atlantic community. The fact that no significant external economic assistance (on the scale of a Marshall Plan) had been provided to help Moscow's post-communist transition was seen as a concrete example of the distance still existing between Russia and the West.[15]

Therefore, since mid-1992, an increasing number of influential foreign policy thinkers and members of the political elite began to call for a new foreign policy, capable of reasserting Russia's role as an 'independent' (from the West) and distinct great power. Eurasianist thought could be seen as gaining positions in the hearts and minds of the foreign policy elite.

The growing influence of the Eurasianists brought about the formation of a new national consensus on foreign policy based on three fundamental principles. First, owing to the uniqueness of its geopolitical position and cultural heritage, Russia's foreign policy cannot be oriented exclusively toward the West. Instead, Russia has to behave as a 'Eurasian' great power. Second, the two overriding priorities of Russia's foreign policy are the preservation of the country's territorial integrity and the maintenance of Russian influence in the 'near abroad' (former Soviet Union). Third, while cooperation with the West is necessary, it should be 'conditional' and based on the principles of 'equality' and recognition of mutual interests.

Principal attention was given to relations with the 'near abroad'. New attempts were made to reconstruct an economic and political space under Russia's hegemony. The territories of the former Soviet Union were officially proclaimed an area of exclusive Russian influence, which paved the way for active Russian military involvement in settling violent conflicts in Georgia, Moldova and Tajikistan. The policy of great power in the 'near abroad' was accompanied by a stronger reliance on the military and by a consolidation of the anti-Western constituencies at home after the 1993 and 1995 parliamentary elections. Moscow's policy of assertiveness culminated in 1994 in the military intervention in Chechnya.

To sum up, contemporary Eurasianism stresses Russia's geopolitical and cultural 'distinctiveness' in contrast with the Westernizers' insistence on Russia's basic affinity with the West. Eurasianism implies that Russia's main priority is control over the former Soviet space, rather than integration with Europe. In the Eurasianist vision of the world, Russia is an independent pole in a global multipolar system, with the right to decide matters of international importance on an equal basis with the other great powers (poles), including Europe, China and Japan.

The tide of Russian foreign policy debates since 1991 has been characterized by the clash between the two different conceptions of Russia's place in the world: one which acknowledges that Russia can be a 'normal' great power by becoming closely integrated to Europe and the West; the other which emphasizes that Russia has a unique identity distinct from the West and can be a great power only by preserving its uniqueness, rather than by following the Western and European path. The present Russian political leadership seeks to combine both of these perspectives in their foreign policies which are marked, above all, by pragmatism

---

Notes

[1] N.S. Trubetzkoy, "Pan-Eurasian Nationalism", in *The Legacy of Ghengis Khan and other Essays on Russia's Identity* (Ann Arbor: Michigan Slavic Publication, 1991), 233.

[2] Sir Halford Mackinder, "The geographical pivot of history", in: *The scope and methods of geography, and The geographical pivot of history*, papers read to the Royal Geographical Society on 31 January 1887, (proceeding of the R.G. S. 9

(1887):141-60) and on 25 January 1904 (Geographical journal 23 (1904): 421-37), reprinted with an introduction by E.W. Gilbert, (London: Royal Geographical Society, 1951).

[3] Martin McCauley, and Peter Waldron, *The Emergence of the Modern Russian State, 1855-81*, (Totowa, NJ: Barnes & Noble Books, 1988) 154.

[4] Ibid, 190.

[5] Hans Kohn, *Pan-Slavism: Its History and Ideology*, (New York: Vintage Books, 1953) 9.

[6] N.S. Trubetzkoy, "Pan-Eurasian Nationalism", in: *The Legacy of Ghengis Khan and other Essays on Russia's Identity*, (Ann Arbor: Michigan Slavic Publication, 1991) 233- 267.

[7] Jesse D. Clarkson, *A History of Russia*, (New York: Random House, 1961) 693.

[8] Graham Fuller, "The next ideology", *Foreign Policy*, Spring 1995, Vol. 14, 34.

[9] Walter Laqueur, *The Dream That Failed: Reflections on the Soviet Union*, (New York: Oxford University Press, 1994) 28.

[10] Leszek Buszynski, *Russian Foreign Policy after the Cold War*, vol. 14 (Westport, CT: Praeger, 1996) 95.

[11] James Richter, "Chapter 4 Russian Foreign Policy and the Politics of National Identity", *The Sources of Russian Foreign Policy after the Cold War*, 213.

[12] Ibid, 80-85.

[13] Richter, 69.

[14] Karen Dawisha, ed, The Making of Foreign Policy in Russia and the New States of Eurasia (Armonk, NY. 1995) 177.

[15] Peter Shearman, ed, *Russian Foreign Policy since 1990*, (Boulder, CO: Westview Press, 1995) 283.

Annex

PROGRAM – RUSSIA: THE CHALLENGE OF CHANGE
Saturday, March 1st, 2003

9 :00 - 9 :20   OPENING REMARKS
Christopher Baker, Kristell Dortel, Eugene Galaev,
Russia Independent Study Committee
Kenneth McRoberts,
Principal, Glendon College; York University

MORNING PANELS
Master of Ceremony
Hon. Barbara McDougall
President & CEO, Canadian Institute of International Affairs,
Former Minister of External Affairs of Canada

9 :20 - 10 :00   *Can Russia Change?*
Robert Johnson
Professor, Department of History, Centre for Russian and East
European Studies, University of Toronto
Presentation: *The Legacy of Change*

Professor Sergei Plekhanov
Associate Professor, Department of Political Science,
Coordinator, Post-Communist Studies Programme,
York University
Presentation: *Who Drives the Troika?*

10 :00 - 11.20   *Problems of Building Democracy in Russia*

Georgi Derluguian
Assistant Professor, Sociology and International Studies,
Northwestern University (Evanston, Illinois)

Peter Solomon
Professor, Department of Political Science, Director, Centre
for Russian and East European Studies, University of Toronto
Presentation: *Reforming Russia's Judiciary*

Valerie Sperling
Assistant Professor, Department of Government,
Clark University (Worcester, Massachusetts)
Presentation: *Engendering Russian Democracy*

11 :20 - 12 :30   *Canada-Russia Relations*

His Excellency, Vitaly Churkin
Ambassador of the Russian Federation to Canada
Presentation: *A Russian View*

Hon. Bill Graham
Minister of Foreign Affairs and International Trade of Canada
Presentation: *A Canadian View*

Anne Leahy
Directeure, Institut des Études internationales de Montréal,
Université du Québec à Montréal,
Former Canadian Ambassador to Russia
Presentation: *Russia Cannot be Fathomed by Reason...*

12 :30 - 1 :45   *Lunch*

PANEL A
Chair
Sergei Plekhanov
Associate Professor, Department of Political Science, Coordinator, Post-Communist Studies Programme, York University

1 :45 - 3:15   **Russia's Post-Communist System**

Georgi Derluguian
Assistant Professor, Sociology and International Studies, Northwestern University (Evanston, Illinois)
Presentation: *Dismantling the Developmental State in Russia: From 1956 to the present*

Joan DeBardeleben
Professor, Department of Political Science, Director, Institute of European and Russian Studies, Carleton University
Presentation: *Russia as a Sum of Parts: Regional Aspects of Transformation*

Piotr Dutkiewicz
Professor, Department of Political Science, Deputy Director, Institute of European and Russian Studies, Carleton University
Presentation: *The Role of Russia's Democracy*

Vladimir Popov
Visiting Professor, Institute of European and Russian Studies, Carleton University
Presentation: *The Russian Economy in the Second Post-Communist Decade*

3:20 - 4:45   **Culture and the Media**

Yevgeni Bai
Izvestia Newspaper Correspondent, Washington D.C.
Presentation: *Is There Freedom of the Press in Russia?*

Natalia Bolotina
Observer, CBC Radio, Toronto.
Presentation: *Development of Information Society*

Richard Pope
Professor Department of Languages, Literature and
Linguistics, York University
Presentation: *Cracking the Enigma Code*

PANEL B
Chair
Stanislav Kirschbaum
Professor, International Studies and Political Science, Glendon College, York
University

1 :45 - 3 :15   *Russia and the World*

Nikolai Zlobin
Director, Russia and Asia Program, Senior FellowCentre for
Defense Information, Washington D.C.
Presentation: *Russia's Place in the Emerging World Order*

Franklyn Griffiths
Professor Emeritus of Political Science; Ignatieff Chair
Emeritus of Peace and Conflict Studies, University of Toronto
Presentation: *Russia: The Case of Plutonium Disposal*

3 :20 - 4 :45   *Doing Business In Russia*

Donald Whalen
President, High River Gold Mines, Ltd.;
President, Canada-Russia Business Forum
Presentation: *Successful Experience: High River Gold*

Alina Pekarsky
Schulich School of Business, York University;
Director, Canada-Russia Business Forum
Presentation: *The Challenge of Transparency*

Nikolai Smirnov
Consul General of the Russian Federation in Toronto
Presentation: *A View From the Russian Side*

5 :00 - 6 :00   *Closing Remarks*